for Natalie!

enjoy!

♥ [signature]

image comics presents

not my bag™

written
and illustrated
by
Sina Grace

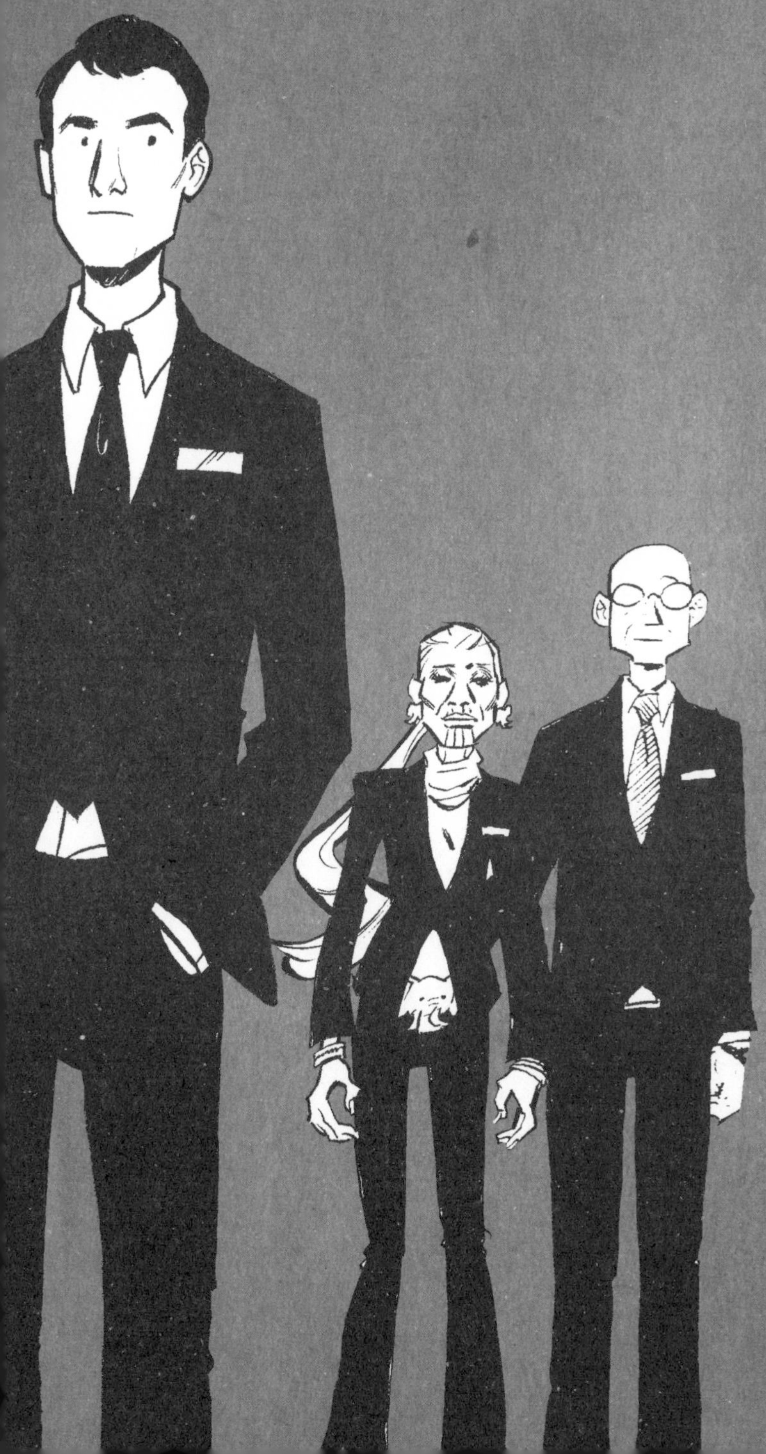

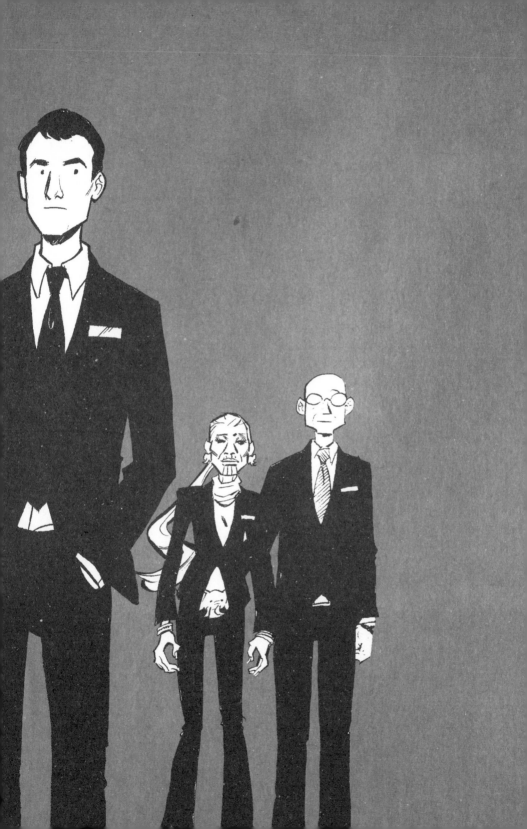

not
my
bag
by Sina Grace

published by Image Comics, Inc.

design:
S. Steven Struble

IMAGE COMICS, INC.
Robert Kirkman - chief operating officer
Erik Larsen - chief financial officer
Todd McFarlane - president
Marc Silvestri - chief executive officer
Jim Valentino - vice-president

Eric Stephenson - publisher
Todd Martinez - sales & licensing coordinator
Jennifer de Guzman - pr & marketing director
Branwyn Bigglestone - accounts manager
Emily Miller - administrative assistant
Jamie Parreno - marketing assistant
Sarah deLaine - events coordinator
Kevin Yuen - digital rights coordinator
Jonathan Chan - production manager
Drew Gill - art director
Monica Garcia - production artist
Vincent Kukua - production artist
Jana Cook - production artist
www.imagecomics.com

NOT MY BAG.
First Printing
ISBN: 978-1-60706-597-5
Published by Image Comics, Inc. Office of publication: 2134 Allston Way, 2nd Floor, Berkeley, CA 94704. Copyright © 2012 Sina Grace. All rights reserved. NOT MY BAG™ the Not My Bag logo and all characters featured in or on this publication and the distinctive names and likenesses thereof, and all related indicia are trademarks of Sina Grace, unless otherwise noted. Image Comics and the Image Comics logos are registered trademarks of Image Comics, Inc. No part of this publication may be reproduced or transmitted in any form or by any means (except for short excerpts for review purposes) without the express written permission of Sina Grace or Image Comics, Inc. No similarity between any of the names, characters, persons, events, and/or institutions in this publication and those of any person or institution is intended (other than for satiric purposes), and any such similarity that may seem to exist is purely coincidental. PRINTED IN SOUTH KOREA.

Representation: Law Offices of Harris M. Miller II, P.C.

dedicated to
Lee Alexander McQueen

prologue

"Death is the sanction of everything the story-teller can tell. He has borrowed his authority from death."

--Walter Benjamin

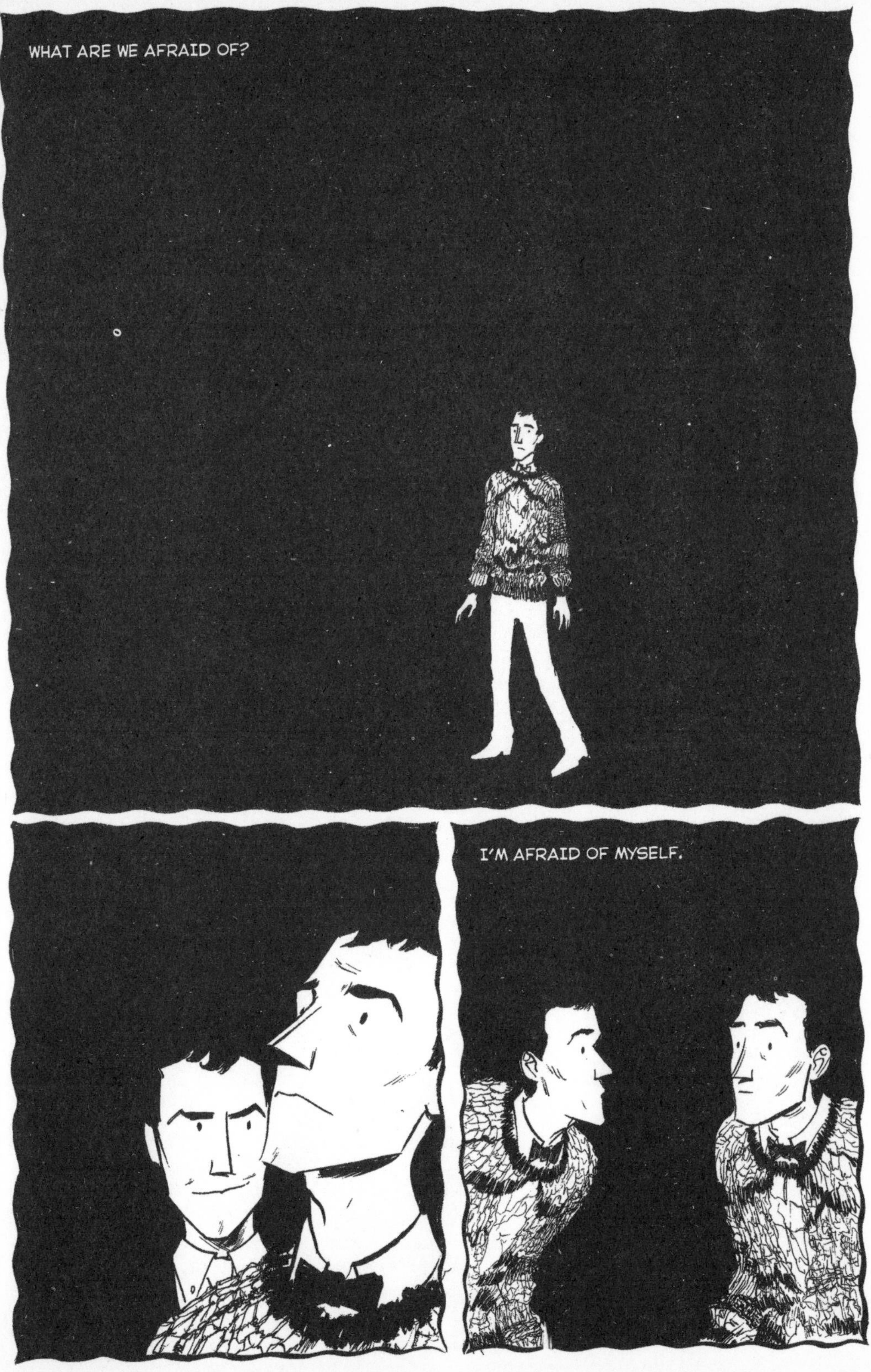
WHAT ARE WE AFRAID OF?
I'M AFRAID OF MYSELF.

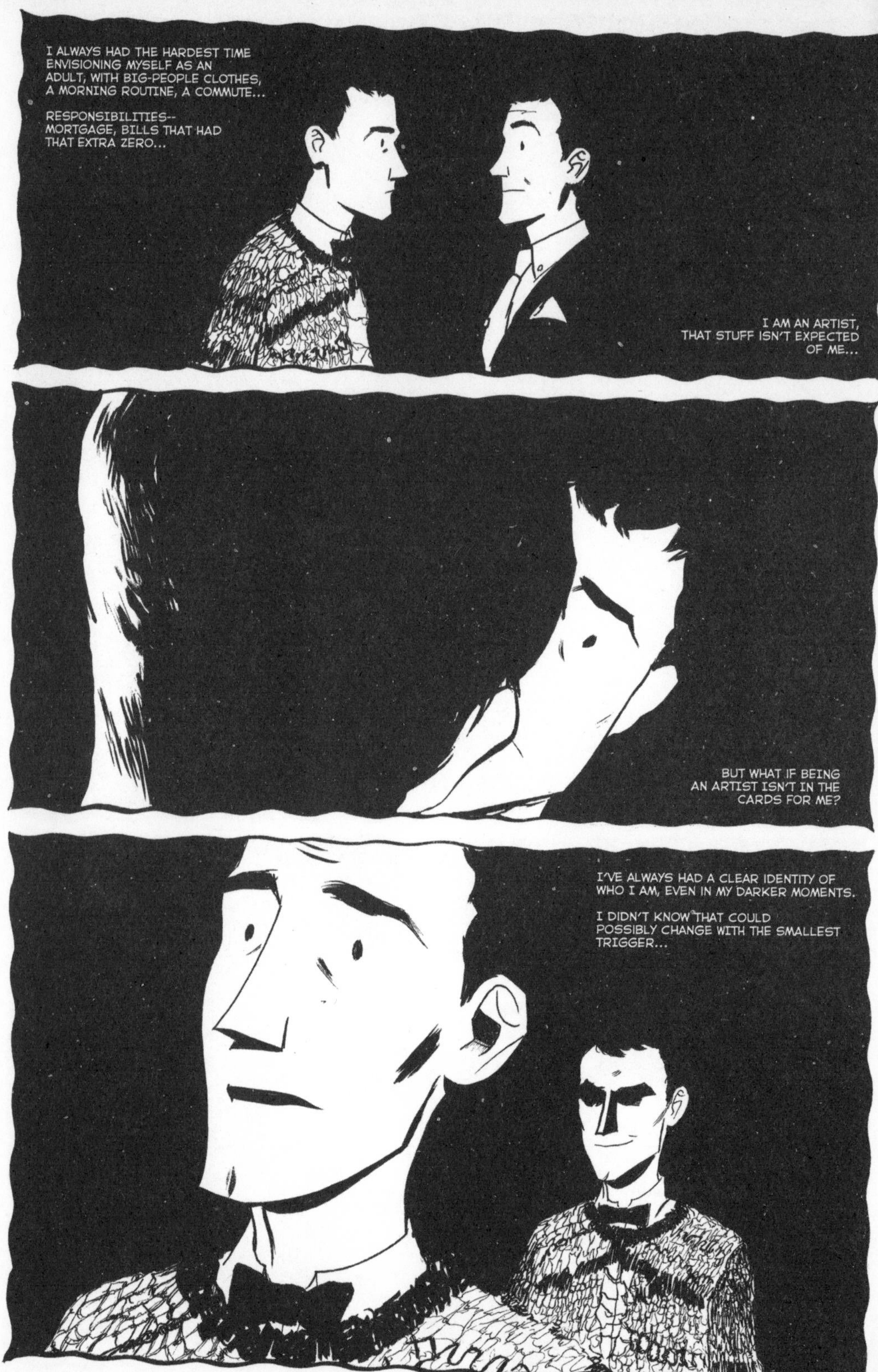
I ALWAYS HAD THE HARDEST TIME ENVISIONING MYSELF AS AN ADULT, WITH BIG-PEOPLE CLOTHES, A MORNING ROUTINE, A COMMUTE...
RESPONSIBILITIES-- MORTGAGE, BILLS THAT HAD THAT EXTRA ZERO...
I AM AN ARTIST, THAT STUFF ISN'T EXPECTED OF ME...
BUT WHAT IF BEING AN ARTIST ISN'T IN THE CARDS FOR ME?
I'VE ALWAYS HAD A CLEAR IDENTITY OF WHO I AM, EVEN IN MY DARKER MOMENTS.
I DIDN'T KNOW THAT COULD POSSIBLY CHANGE WITH THE SMALLEST TRIGGER...

chapter one

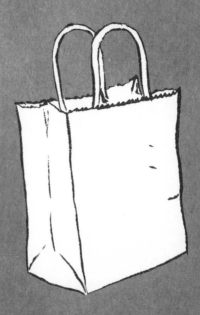

"I'm about what goes
through people's minds,
the stuff that people don't
want to admit or face up
to. The shows are about
what's buried in people's
psyches."

--Alexander McQueen

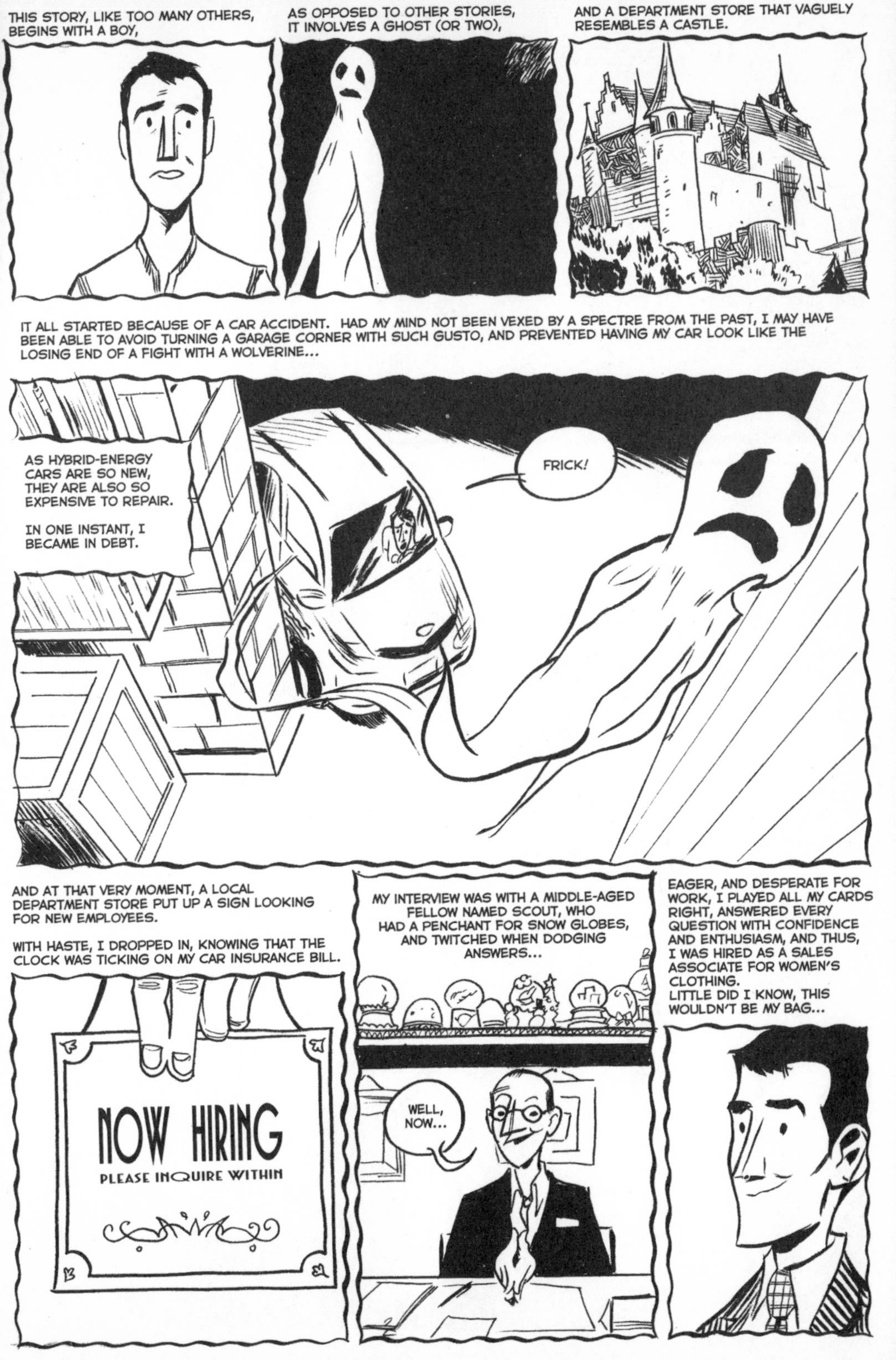
THIS STORY, LIKE TOO MANY OTHERS, BEGINS WITH A BOY,
AS OPPOSED TO OTHER STORIES, IT INVOLVES A GHOST (OR TWO),
AND A DEPARTMENT STORE THAT VAGUELY RESEMBLES A CASTLE.
IT ALL STARTED BECAUSE OF A CAR ACCIDENT. HAD MY MIND NOT BEEN VEXED BY A SPECTRE FROM THE PAST, I MAY HAVE BEEN ABLE TO AVOID TURNING A GARAGE CORNER WITH SUCH GUSTO, AND PREVENTED HAVING MY CAR LOOK LIKE THE LOSING END OF A FIGHT WITH A WOLVERINE...
AS HYBRID-ENERGY CARS ARE SO NEW, THEY ARE ALSO SO EXPENSIVE TO REPAIR.
IN ONE INSTANT, I BECAME IN DEBT.
FRICK!
AND AT THAT VERY MOMENT, A LOCAL DEPARTMENT STORE PUT UP A SIGN LOOKING FOR NEW EMPLOYEES.
WITH HASTE, I DROPPED IN, KNOWING THAT THE CLOCK WAS TICKING ON MY CAR INSURANCE BILL.
NOW HIRING
PLEASE INQUIRE WITHIN
MY INTERVIEW WAS WITH A MIDDLE-AGED FELLOW NAMED SCOUT, WHO HAD A PENCHANT FOR SNOW GLOBES, AND TWITCHED WHEN DODGING ANSWERS...
WELL, NOW...
EAGER, AND DESPERATE FOR WORK, I PLAYED ALL MY CARDS RIGHT, ANSWERED EVERY QUESTION WITH CONFIDENCE AND ENTHUSIASM, AND THUS, I WAS HIRED AS A SALES ASSOCIATE FOR WOMEN'S CLOTHING.
LITTLE DID I KNOW, THIS WOULDN'T BE MY BAG...

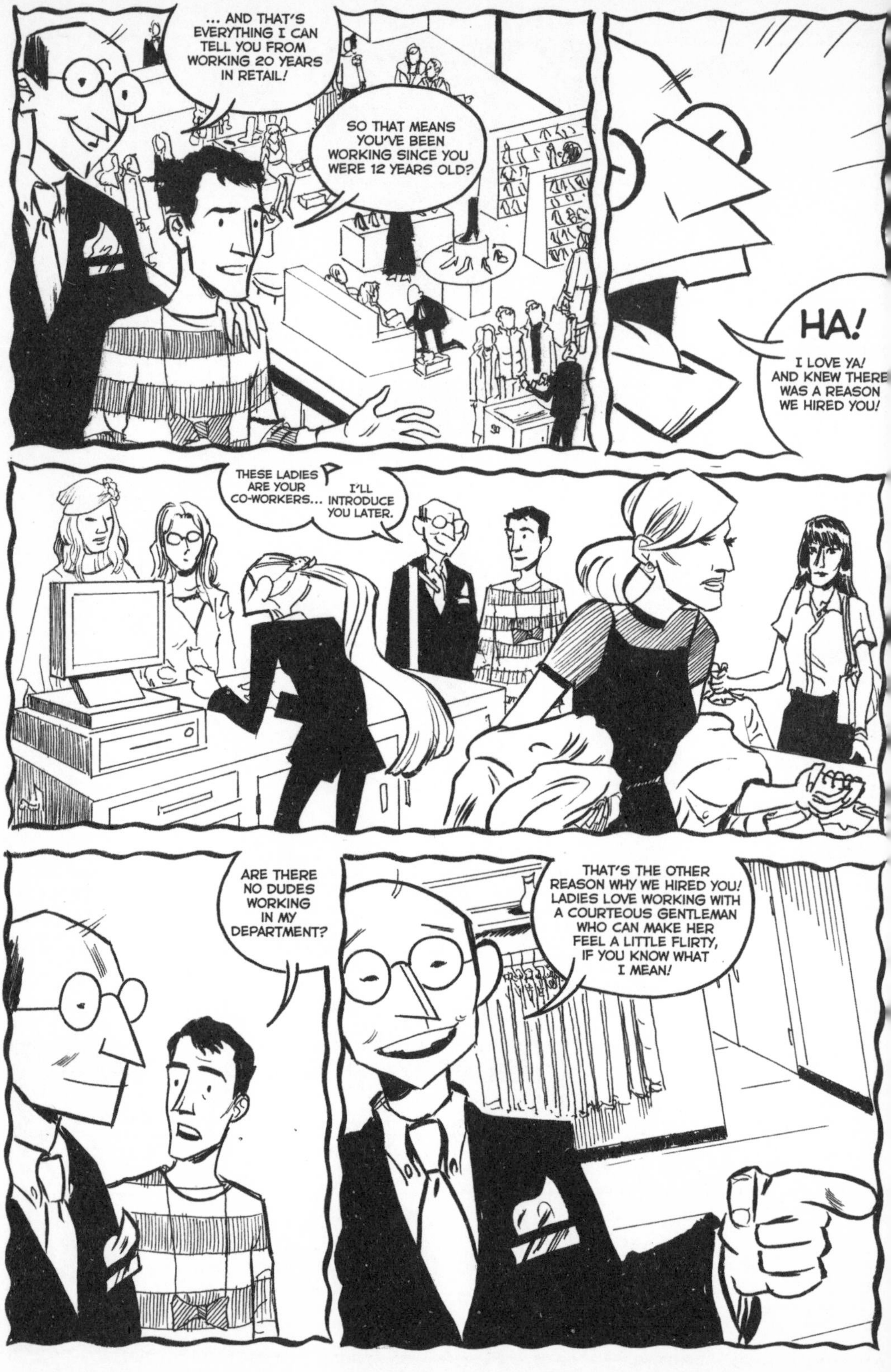
... AND THAT'S EVERYTHING I CAN TELL YOU FROM WORKING 20 YEARS IN RETAIL!
SO THAT MEANS YOU'VE BEEN WORKING SINCE YOU WERE 12 YEARS OLD?
HA!
I LOVE YA! AND KNEW THERE WAS A REASON WE HIRED YOU!
THESE LADIES ARE YOUR CO-WORKERS...
I'LL INTRODUCE YOU LATER.
ARE THERE NO DUDES WORKING IN MY DEPARTMENT?
THAT'S THE OTHER REASON WHY WE HIRED YOU! LADIES LOVE WORKING WITH A COURTEOUS GENTLEMAN WHO CAN MAKE HER FEEL A LITTLE FLIRTY, IF YOU KNOW WHAT I MEAN!

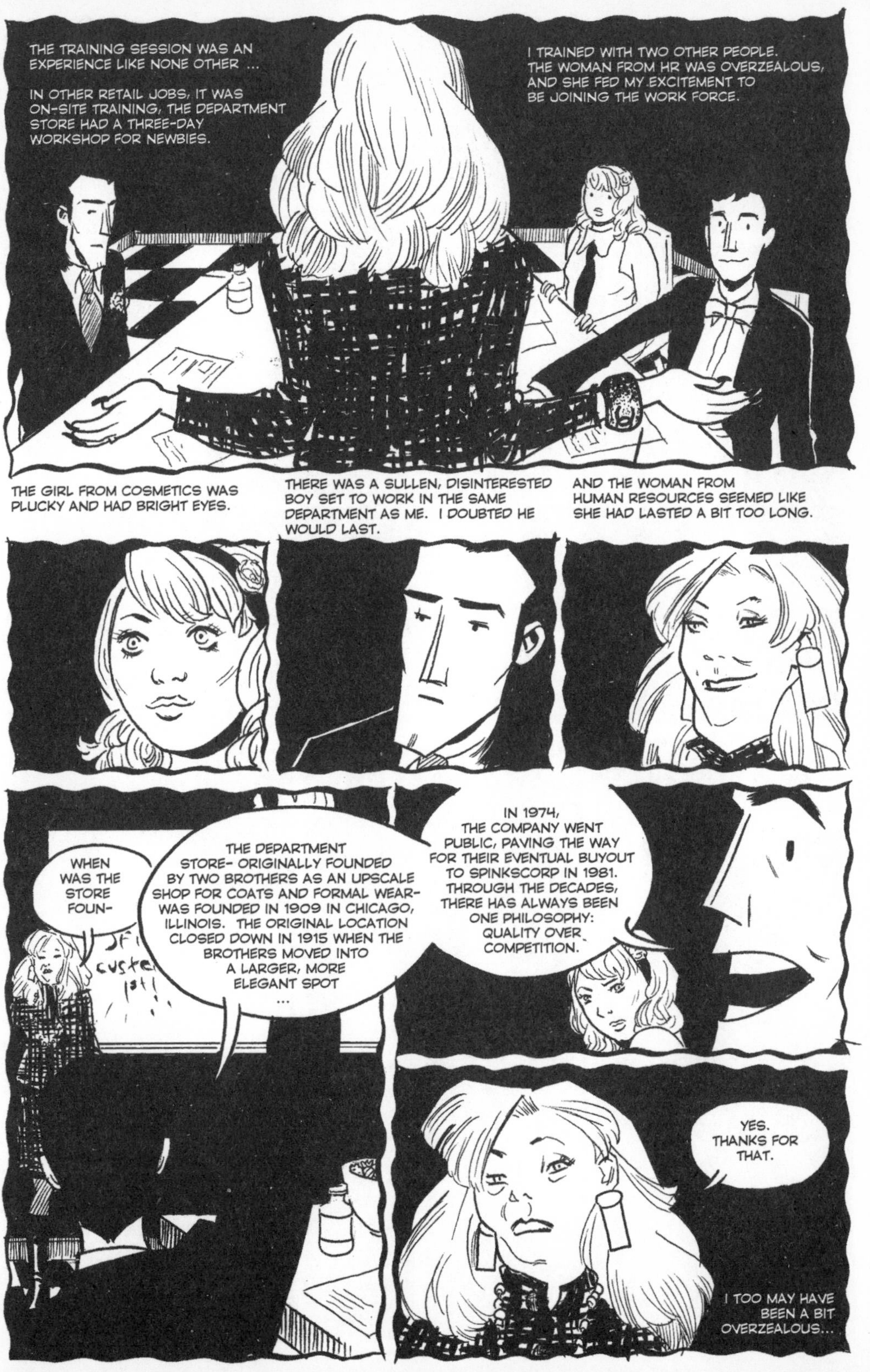
THE TRAINING SESSION WAS AN EXPERIENCE LIKE NONE OTHER ...
IN OTHER RETAIL JOBS, IT WAS ON-SITE TRAINING, THE DEPARTMENT STORE HAD A THREE-DAY WORKSHOP FOR NEWBIES.
I TRAINED WITH TWO OTHER PEOPLE. THE WOMAN FROM HR WAS OVERZEALOUS, AND SHE FED MY EXCITEMENT TO BE JOINING THE WORK FORCE.
THE GIRL FROM COSMETICS WAS PLUCKY AND HAD BRIGHT EYES.
THERE WAS A SULLEN, DISINTERESTED BOY SET TO WORK IN THE SAME DEPARTMENT AS ME. I DOUBTED HE WOULD LAST.
AND THE WOMAN FROM HUMAN RESOURCES SEEMED LIKE SHE HAD LASTED A BIT TOO LONG.
WHEN WAS THE STORE FOUN-
THE DEPARTMENT STORE- ORIGINALLY FOUNDED BY TWO BROTHERS AS AN UPSCALE SHOP FOR COATS AND FORMAL WEAR- WAS FOUNDED IN 1909 IN CHICAGO, ILLINOIS. THE ORIGINAL LOCATION CLOSED DOWN IN 1915 WHEN THE BROTHERS MOVED INTO A LARGER, MORE ELEGANT SPOT ...
IN 1974, THE COMPANY WENT PUBLIC, PAVING THE WAY FOR THEIR EVENTUAL BUYOUT TO SPINKSCORP IN 1981. THROUGH THE DECADES, THERE HAS ALWAYS BEEN ONE PHILOSOPHY: QUALITY OVER COMPETITION.
YES. THANKS FOR THAT.
I TOO MAY HAVE BEEN A BIT OVERZEALOUS...

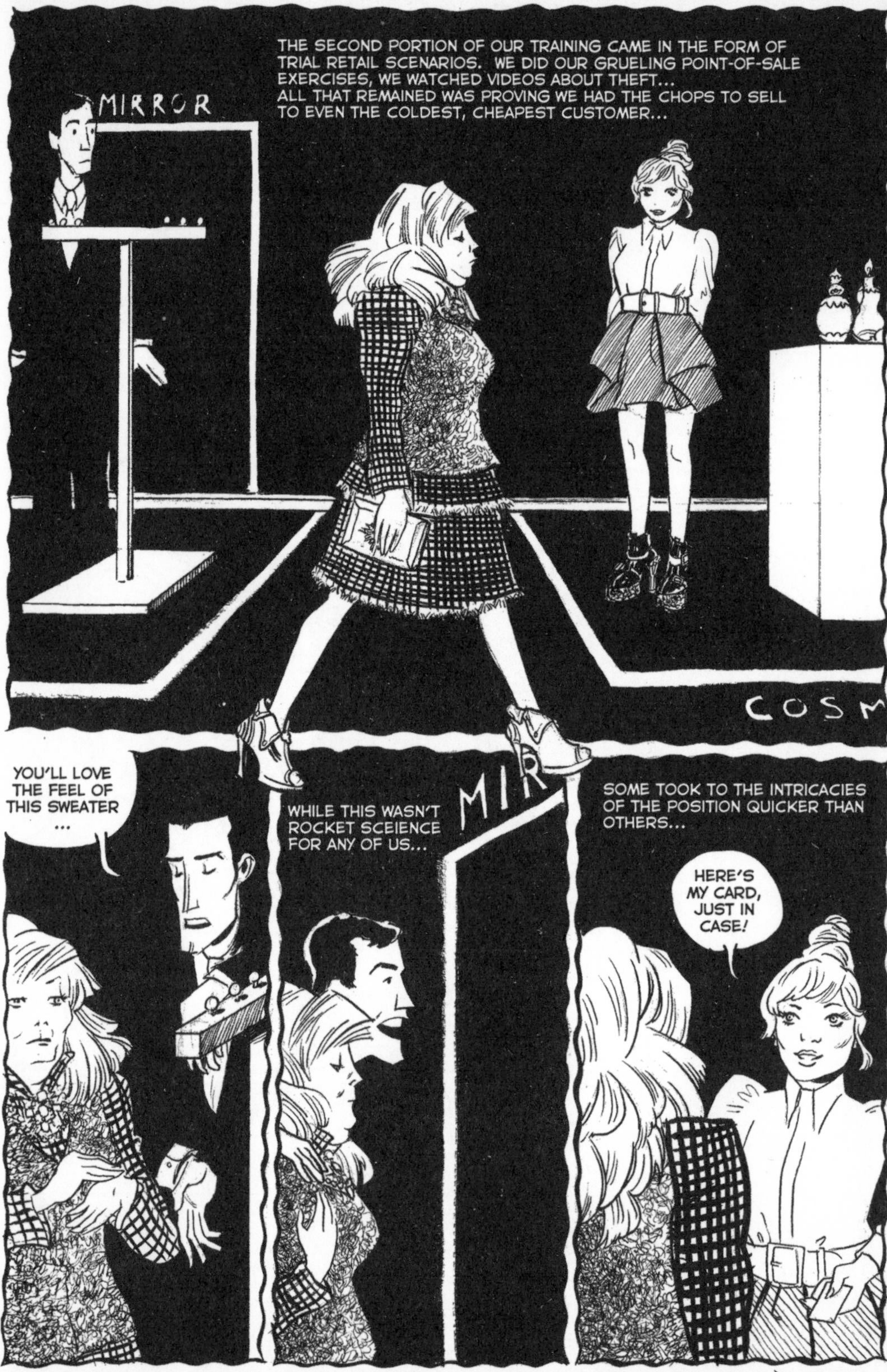
THE SECOND PORTION OF OUR TRAINING CAME IN THE FORM OF TRIAL RETAIL SCENARIOS. WE DID OUR GRUELING POINT-OF-SALE EXERCISES, WE WATCHED VIDEOS ABOUT THEFT...
ALL THAT REMAINED WAS PROVING WE HAD THE CHOPS TO SELL TO EVEN THE COLDEST, CHEAPEST CUSTOMER...
MIRROR
COSM
YOU'LL LOVE THE FEEL OF THIS SWEATER ...
WHILE THIS WASN'T ROCKET SCEIENCE FOR ANY OF US...
MIR
SOME TOOK TO THE INTRICACIES OF THE POSITION QUICKER THAN OTHERS...
HERE'S MY CARD, JUST IN CASE!

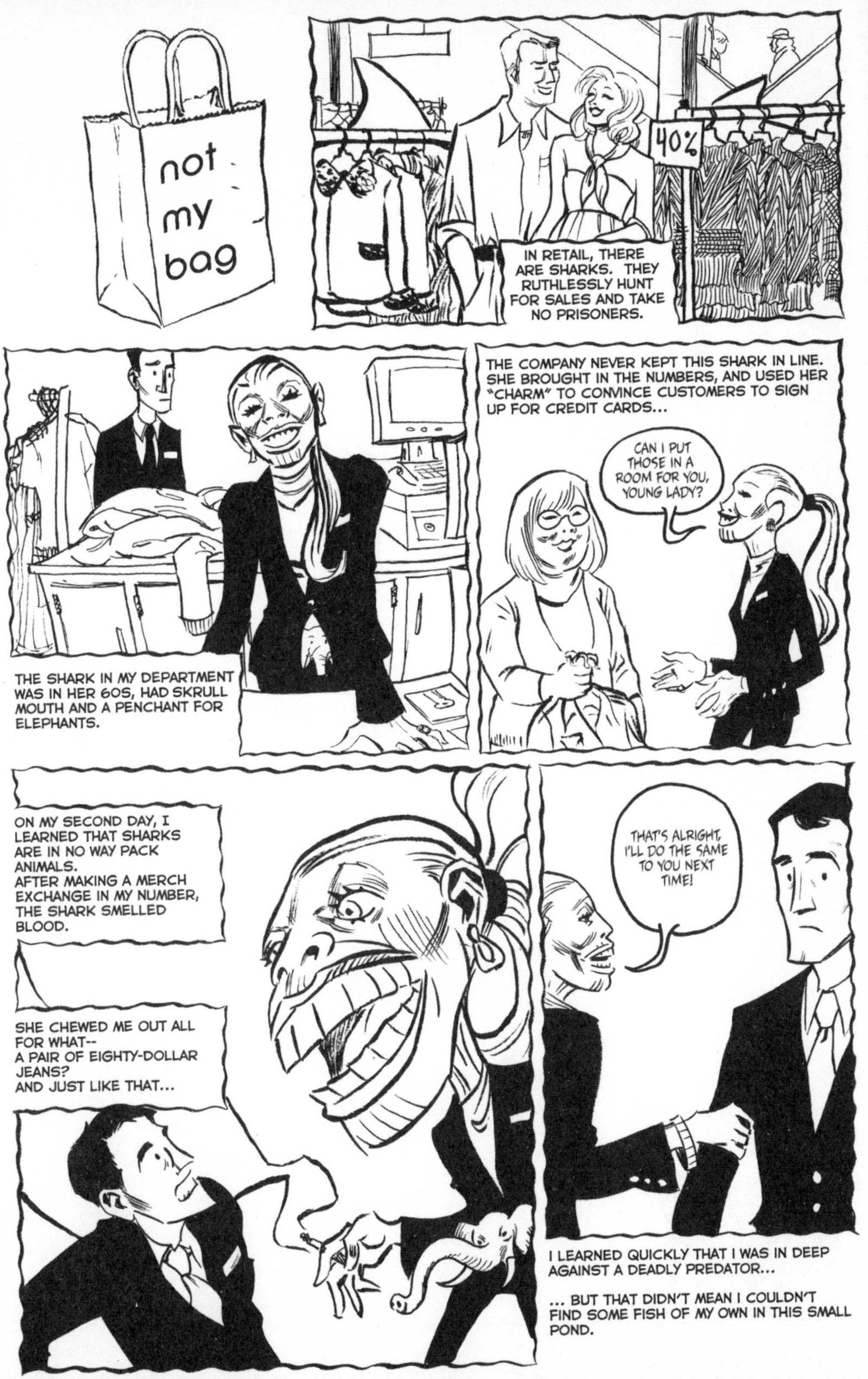
not my bag
40%
IN RETAIL, THERE ARE SHARKS. THEY RUTHLESSLY HUNT FOR SALES AND TAKE NO PRISONERS.
THE SHARK IN MY DEPARTMENT WAS IN HER 60S, HAD SKRULL MOUTH AND A PENCHANT FOR ELEPHANTS.
THE COMPANY NEVER KEPT THIS SHARK IN LINE. SHE BROUGHT IN THE NUMBERS, AND USED HER "CHARM" TO CONVINCE CUSTOMERS TO SIGN UP FOR CREDIT CARDS...
CAN I PUT THOSE IN A ROOM FOR YOU, YOUNG LADY?
ON MY SECOND DAY, I LEARNED THAT SHARKS ARE IN NO WAY PACK ANIMALS. AFTER MAKING A MERCH EXCHANGE IN MY NUMBER, THE SHARK SMELLED BLOOD.
SHE CHEWED ME OUT ALL FOR WHAT-- A PAIR OF EIGHTY-DOLLAR JEANS? AND JUST LIKE THAT...
THAT'S ALRIGHT, I'LL DO THE SAME TO YOU NEXT TIME!
I LEARNED QUICKLY THAT I WAS IN DEEP AGAINST A DEADLY PREDATOR...
... BUT THAT DIDN'T MEAN I COULDN'T FIND SOME FISH OF MY OWN IN THIS SMALL POND.

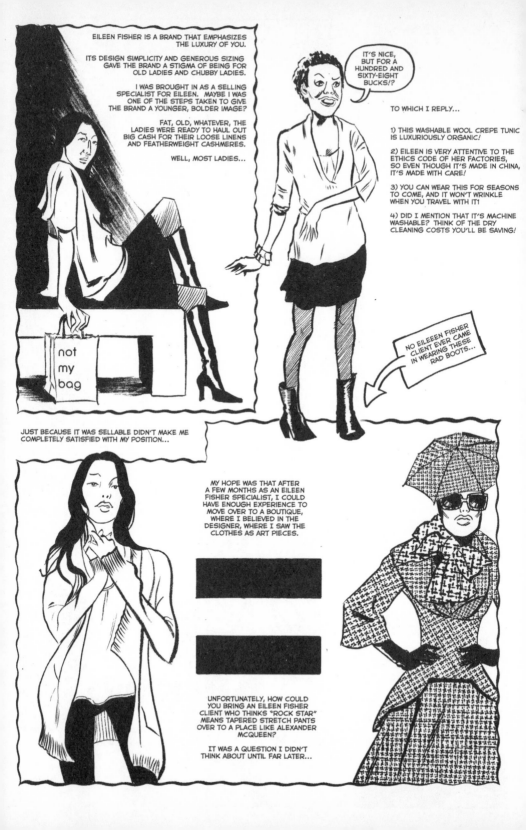

EILEEN FISHER IS A BRAND THAT EMPHASIZES THE LUXURY OF YOU.

ITS DESIGN SIMPLICITY AND GENEROUS SIZING GAVE THE BRAND A STIGMA OF BEING FOR OLD LADIES AND CHUBBY LADIES.

I WAS BROUGHT IN AS A SELLING SPECIALIST FOR EILEEN. MAYBE I WAS ONE OF THE STEPS TAKEN TO GIVE THE BRAND A YOUNGER, BOLDER IMAGE?

FAT, OLD, WHATEVER, THE LADIES WERE READY TO HAUL OUT BIG CASH FOR THEIR LOOSE LINENS AND FEATHERWEIGHT CASHMERES.

WELL, MOST LADIES...

not my bag

IT'S NICE, BUT FOR A HUNDRED AND SIXTY-EIGHT BUCKS!?

TO WHICH I REPLY...

1) THIS WASHABLE WOOL CREPE TUNIC IS LUXURIOUSLY ORGANIC!

2) EILEEN IS VERY ATTENTIVE TO THE ETHICS CODE OF HER FACTORIES, SO EVEN THOUGH IT'S MADE IN CHINA, IT'S MADE WITH CARE!

3) YOU CAN WEAR THIS FOR SEASONS TO COME, AND IT WON'T WRINKLE WHEN YOU TRAVEL WITH IT!

4) DID I MENTION THAT IT'S MACHINE WASHABLE? THINK OF THE DRY CLEANING COSTS YOU'LL BE SAVING!

NO EILEEN FISHER CLIENT EVER CAME IN WEARING THESE RAD BOOTS...

JUST BECAUSE IT WAS SELLABLE DIDN'T MAKE ME COMPLETELY SATISFIED WITH MY POSITION...

MY HOPE WAS THAT AFTER A FEW MONTHS AS AN EILEEN FISHER SPECIALIST, I COULD HAVE ENOUGH EXPERIENCE TO MOVE OVER TO A BOUTIQUE, WHERE I BELIEVED IN THE DESIGNER, WHERE I SAW THE CLOTHES AS ART PIECES.

UNFORTUNATELY, HOW COULD YOU BRING AN EILEEN FISHER CLIENT WHO THINKS "ROCK STAR" MEANS TAPERED STRETCH PANTS OVER TO A PLACE LIKE ALEXANDER MCQUEEN?

IT WAS A QUESTION I DIDN'T THINK ABOUT UNTIL FAR LATER...

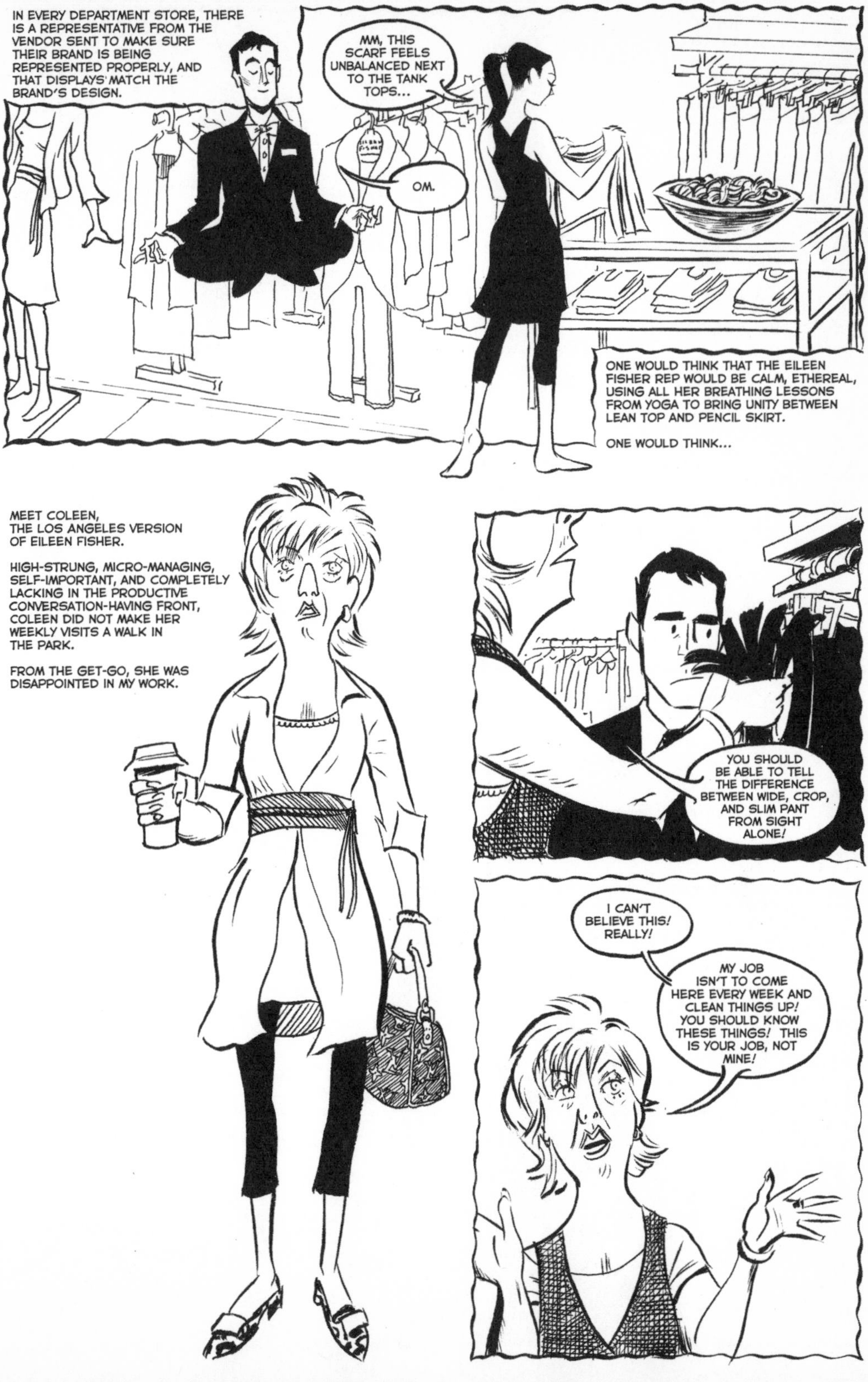
IN EVERY DEPARTMENT STORE, THERE IS A REPRESENTATIVE FROM THE VENDOR SENT TO MAKE SURE THEIR BRAND IS BEING REPRESENTED PROPERLY, AND THAT DISPLAYS MATCH THE BRAND'S DESIGN.
MM, THIS SCARF FEELS UNBALANCED NEXT TO THE TANK TOPS...
OM.
ONE WOULD THINK THAT THE EILEEN FISHER REP WOULD BE CALM, ETHEREAL, USING ALL HER BREATHING LESSONS FROM YOGA TO BRING UNITY BETWEEN LEAN TOP AND PENCIL SKIRT.
ONE WOULD THINK...
MEET COLEEN, THE LOS ANGELES VERSION OF EILEEN FISHER.
HIGH-STRUNG, MICRO-MANAGING, SELF-IMPORTANT, AND COMPLETELY LACKING IN THE PRODUCTIVE CONVERSATION-HAVING FRONT, COLEEN DID NOT MAKE HER WEEKLY VISITS A WALK IN THE PARK.
FROM THE GET-GO, SHE WAS DISAPPOINTED IN MY WORK.
YOU SHOULD BE ABLE TO TELL THE DIFFERENCE BETWEEN WIDE, CROP, AND SLIM PANT FROM SIGHT ALONE!
I CAN'T BELIEVE THIS! REALLY!
MY JOB ISN'T TO COME HERE EVERY WEEK AND CLEAN THINGS UP! YOU SHOULD KNOW THESE THINGS! THIS IS YOUR JOB, NOT MINE!

IN SOME WAYS, SHE WAS RIGHT.

EVEN THOUGH I DIDN'T QUITE KNOW WHAT I WAS GETTING INTO, I HAD SIGNED A CONTRACT WITH EILEEN FISHER, AND IN TRADE FOR MY FAIR SHARE OF FREE WORK SHIRTS AND NECKTIES, I HAD TO EXCEL IN PRODUCT KNOWLEDGE.

RATHER THAN CONCEDE DEFEAT OR GIVE UP, I DID ALL THAT I COULD DO TO LEARN MORE ABOUT THE CLOTHES, SHORT OF JUMPING INTO A FITTING ROOM AND TRYING THEM ON.

IT TURNED OUT, THERE WAS A WAY TO RECOGNIZE THE DIFFERENCE BETWEEN TWO BLACK STRETCH PANTS BY LOOK ALONE.

BY SCOURING THE BACK STOCK AND PERFORMING A REPLENISHMENT CHECK, I NOT ONLY HAD ENOUGH OF EVERY SIZE OUT ON THE FLOOR, BUT NOTHING SEEMED DAUNTING.

ALL I HAD TO DO WAS APPLY MYSELF. I TREATED MY JOB LIKE I WAS COLLECTING COMICS, AND LIKENED REMEMBERING THE MANY WAYS OF SAYING "GRAY" ("ASH," "CHARCOAL," "DARK PEARL," "SILVER") TO THE DIFFERENT WAYS YOU COULD CALL A VARIANT COVER "SHINY" ("LENTICULAR," "PRISMATIC," "HOLOFOIL," AND SO ON).

SLOWLY BUT SURELY, I BEGAN TO SPEAK OF THE EILEEN FISHER PRODUCT WITH THE SAME INDIGNANT AUTHORITY AS COLEEN HERSELF.

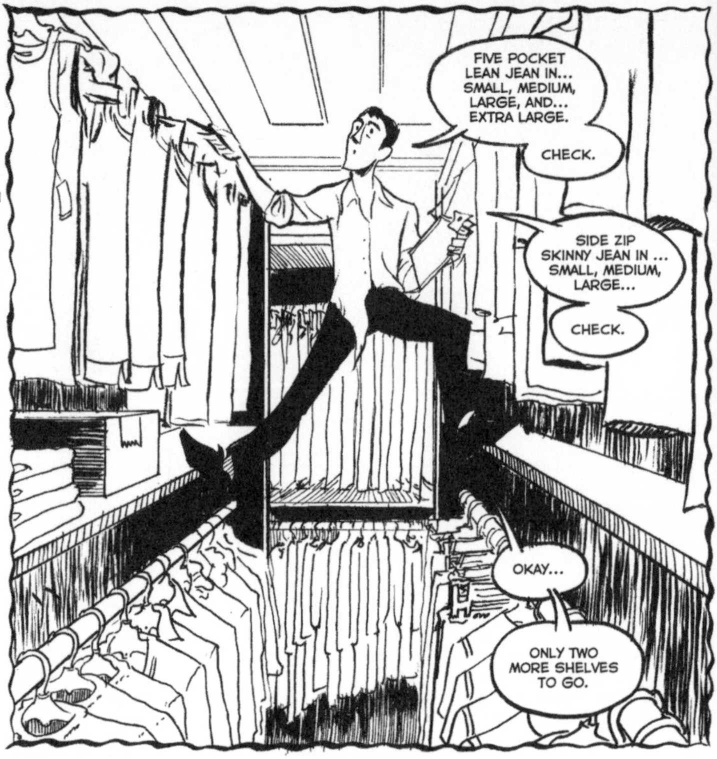
FIVE POCKET LEAN JEAN IN... SMALL, MEDIUM, LARGE, AND... EXTRA LARGE.
CHECK.
SIDE ZIP SKINNY JEAN IN ... SMALL, MEDIUM, LARGE...
CHECK.
OKAY...
ONLY TWO MORE SHELVES TO GO.

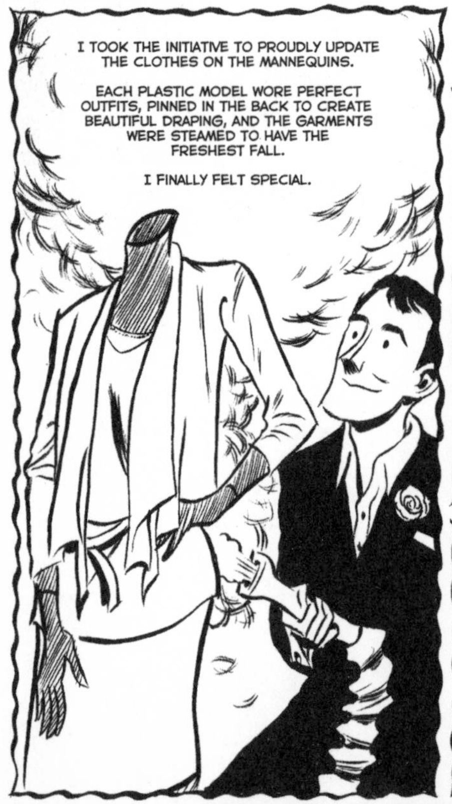
I TOOK THE INITIATIVE TO PROUDLY UPDATE THE CLOTHES ON THE MANNEQUINS.
EACH PLASTIC MODEL WORE PERFECT OUTFITS, PINNED IN THE BACK TO CREATE BEAUTIFUL DRAPING, AND THE GARMENTS WERE STEAMED TO HAVE THE FRESHEST FALL.
I FINALLY FELT SPECIAL.

UPON COLEEN'S ARRIVAL, I WALKED THE FLOOR WITH TREPIDATION, CERTAIN THAT I MISSED SOMETHING IN OUR PHONE CALL THE DAY PRIOR (I DID THIS AS A MEANS TO MANAGE HER EXPECTATIONS). BUT THE HARD WORK PAID OFF...

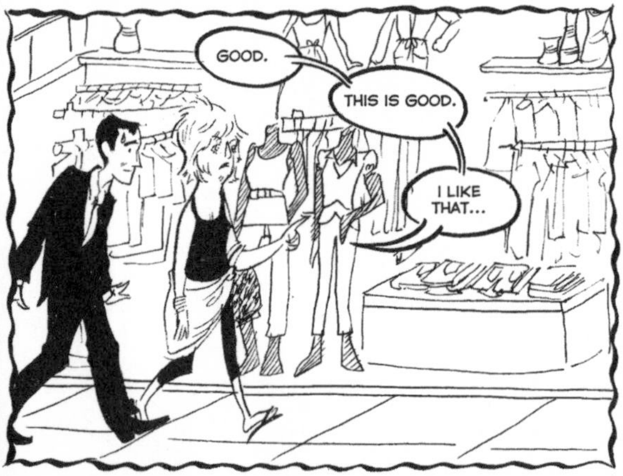
GOOD.
THIS IS GOOD.
I LIKE THAT...

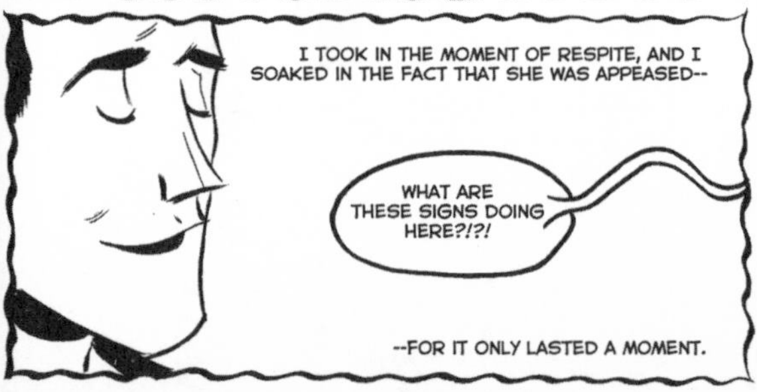
I TOOK IN THE MOMENT OF RESPITE, AND I SOAKED IN THE FACT THAT SHE WAS APPEASED--
WHAT ARE THESE SIGNS DOING HERE?!?!
--FOR IT ONLY LASTED A MOMENT.

$10.13 /hr
draw
+
commission

EVERYBODY KNOWS THAT IN HIGHER-END RETAIL, THE SALES PEOPLE WORK ON COMMISSION. WHY ELSE WOULD THERE BE SHARKS, RIGHT? EACH COMPANY HAS A DIFFERENT WAY OF BREAKING IT DOWN FOR THEIR EMPLOYEES. MY SET-UP WAS ONE WHERE IT SOUNDED LIKE THEY WERE DOING US A HUGE FAVOR, BUT IT FELT MORE LIKE DOING HIGH SCHOOL ALGEBRA...

SO, IT BREAKS DOWN LIKE THIS: I AM GUARANTEED TEN BUCKS AND SOME CHANGE FROM THE COMPANY, THEY'LL PAY ME THAT NO MATTER WHAT. IN RETURN, HOWEVER... THEY WANT ME TO SELL ABOUT $1,500 IN MERCHANDISE DAILY BEFORE I CAN FACTOR GETTING ANY COMMISSION ON TOP OF THAT. AN EFFECTIVE BUSINESS MODEL? MAYBE FOR THE COMPANY, BUT TAKE A LOOK AT HOW IT PLAYS OUT FOR THE SALESPERSON.

AFTER THE $1,500 IN SALES, ONE FINALLY GETS ACCESS TO A 6.75% COMMISSION RATE. IF I END A DAY WITH TWO GRAND IN SALES, I GET COMMISSION ON $500 OF THAT. NOW THINK OF THIS: IF I GET A RETURN ON A DAY WHERE I HAVE CRUMMY SALES, THEN I'M IN DEFICIT- MEANING THAT I OWE THE COMPANY MONEY. BLERG.

THE GOOD

I'M ON LUNCH SO RING ME UP QUICK.

AND I KNOW MY SIZE SO I WON'T BE COMING BACK.

THE WAIT

OKAY, SO IF IT'S TWO WEEKS 'TIL MY COMMISSION COMES IN, THEN I WILL BE GETTING $200 THIS WEEK, CARRY THE SALE OVER AND..

FITTING ROOM, PLEASE!

THE BAD

I'M JUST LOOKING, THANKS.

FIT WASN'T RIGHT.

THE RETURN

I JUST LOST MY JOB, SO I NEED TO CUT BACK!

MY HUSBAND THINKS THAT THE TOP MAKES ME LOOK LIKE A SWOLLEN PIMPLE. SORRY!

YOUNGER CUSTOMERS

GOTTA GO, PEOPLE ARE STARTING TO LINE UP. I'LL CALL LATER.

THE HEM NEEDS TO BE A BIT HIGHER.

HMM...

GIVE ME THE TAILOR'S DIRECT LINE. OR CELL PHONE.

MY CUSTOMERS

THE RESULT

A VERY TUCKERED-OUT ARTIST WHO WORKS VERY HARD FOR AN INCREDIBLY MOODY PAYCHECK.

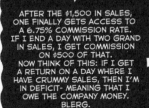

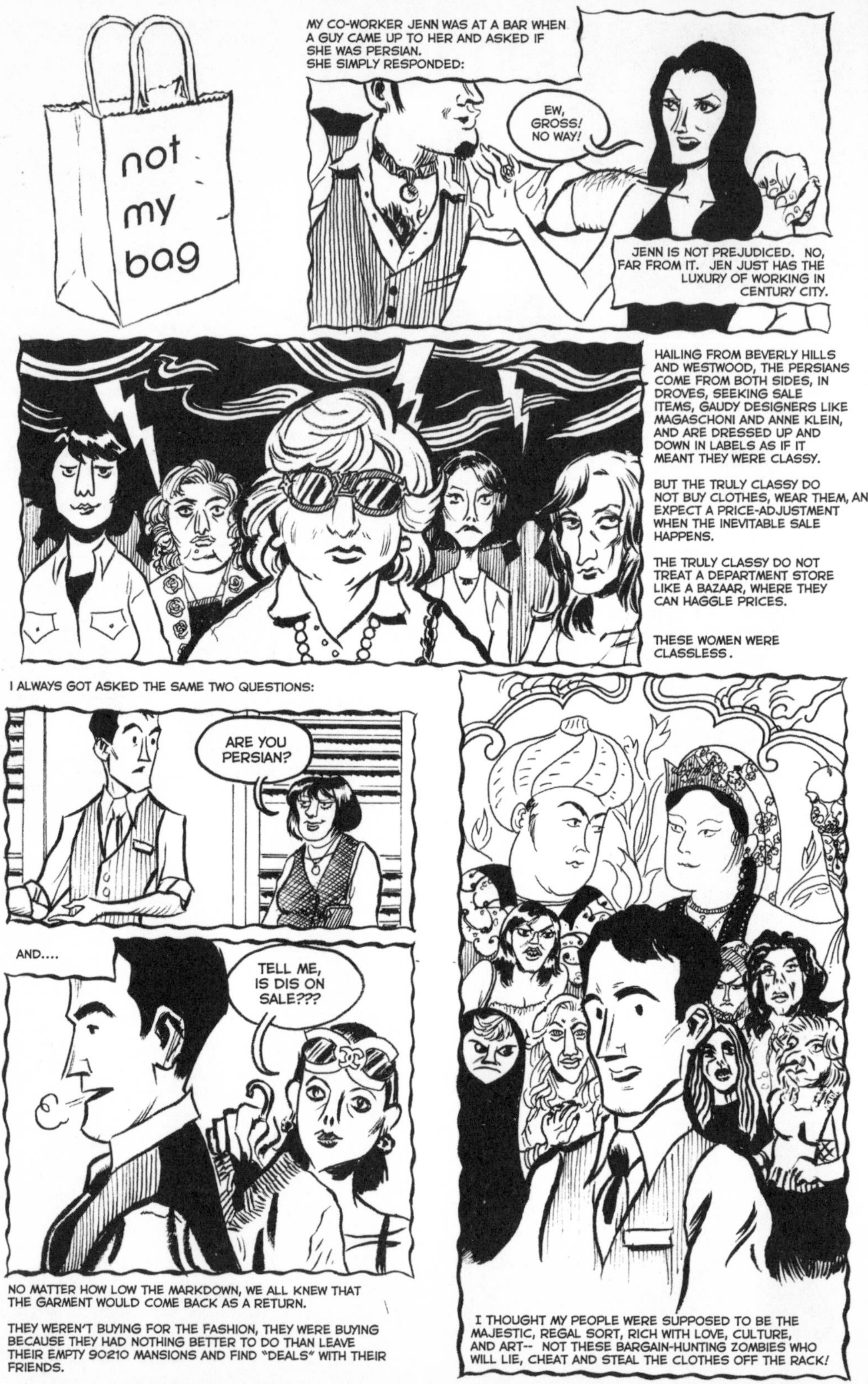
not my bag
MY CO-WORKER JENN WAS AT A BAR WHEN A GUY CAME UP TO HER AND ASKED IF SHE WAS PERSIAN. SHE SIMPLY RESPONDED:
EW, GROSS! NO WAY!
JENN IS NOT PREJUDICED. NO, FAR FROM IT. JEN JUST HAS THE LUXURY OF WORKING IN CENTURY CITY.
HAILING FROM BEVERLY HILLS AND WESTWOOD, THE PERSIANS COME FROM BOTH SIDES, IN DROVES, SEEKING SALE ITEMS, GAUDY DESIGNERS LIKE MAGASCHONI AND ANNE KLEIN, AND ARE DRESSED UP AND DOWN IN LABELS AS IF IT MEANT THEY WERE CLASSY.
BUT THE TRULY CLASSY DO NOT BUY CLOTHES, WEAR THEM, AND EXPECT A PRICE-ADJUSTMENT WHEN THE INEVITABLE SALE HAPPENS.
THE TRULY CLASSY DO NOT TREAT A DEPARTMENT STORE LIKE A BAZAAR, WHERE THEY CAN HAGGLE PRICES.
THESE WOMEN WERE CLASSLESS.
I ALWAYS GOT ASKED THE SAME TWO QUESTIONS:
ARE YOU PERSIAN?
AND....
TELL ME, IS DIS ON SALE???
NO MATTER HOW LOW THE MARKDOWN, WE ALL KNEW THAT THE GARMENT WOULD COME BACK AS A RETURN.
THEY WEREN'T BUYING FOR THE FASHION, THEY WERE BUYING BECAUSE THEY HAD NOTHING BETTER TO DO THAN LEAVE THEIR EMPTY 90210 MANSIONS AND FIND "DEALS" WITH THEIR FRIENDS.
I THOUGHT MY PEOPLE WERE SUPPOSED TO BE THE MAJESTIC, REGAL SORT, RICH WITH LOVE, CULTURE, AND ART-- NOT THESE BARGAIN-HUNTING ZOMBIES WHO WILL LIE, CHEAT AND STEAL THE CLOTHES OFF THE RACK!

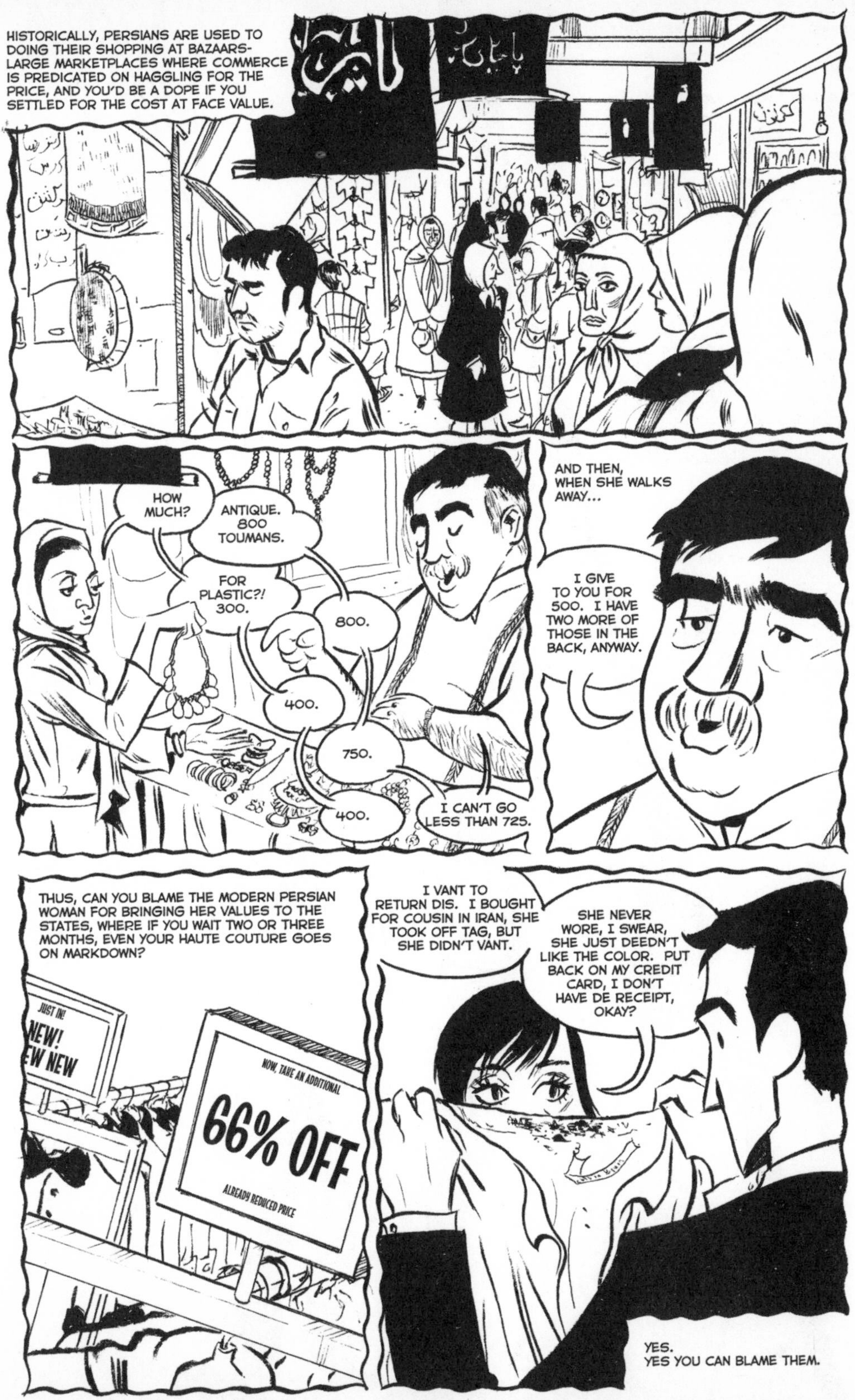

HISTORICALLY, PERSIANS ARE USED TO DOING THEIR SHOPPING AT BAZAARS- LARGE MARKETPLACES WHERE COMMERCE IS PREDICATED ON HAGGLING FOR THE PRICE, AND YOU'D BE A DOPE IF YOU SETTLED FOR THE COST AT FACE VALUE.
HOW MUCH?
ANTIQUE. 800 TOUMANS.
FOR PLASTIC?! 300.
800.
400.
750.
400.
I CAN'T GO LESS THAN 725.
AND THEN, WHEN SHE WALKS AWAY...
I GIVE TO YOU FOR 500. I HAVE TWO MORE OF THOSE IN THE BACK, ANYWAY.
THUS, CAN YOU BLAME THE MODERN PERSIAN WOMAN FOR BRINGING HER VALUES TO THE STATES, WHERE IF YOU WAIT TWO OR THREE MONTHS, EVEN YOUR HAUTE COUTURE GOES ON MARKDOWN?
JUST IN!
NEW!
EW NEW
NOW, TAKE AN ADDITIONAL
66% OFF
ALREADY REDUCED PRICE
I VANT TO RETURN DIS. I BOUGHT FOR COUSIN IN IRAN, SHE TOOK OFF TAG, BUT SHE DIDN'T VANT.
SHE NEVER WORE, I SWEAR, SHE JUST DEEDN'T LIKE THE COLOR. PUT BACK ON MY CREDIT CARD, I DON'T HAVE DE RECEIPT, OKAY?
YES.
YES YOU CAN BLAME THEM.

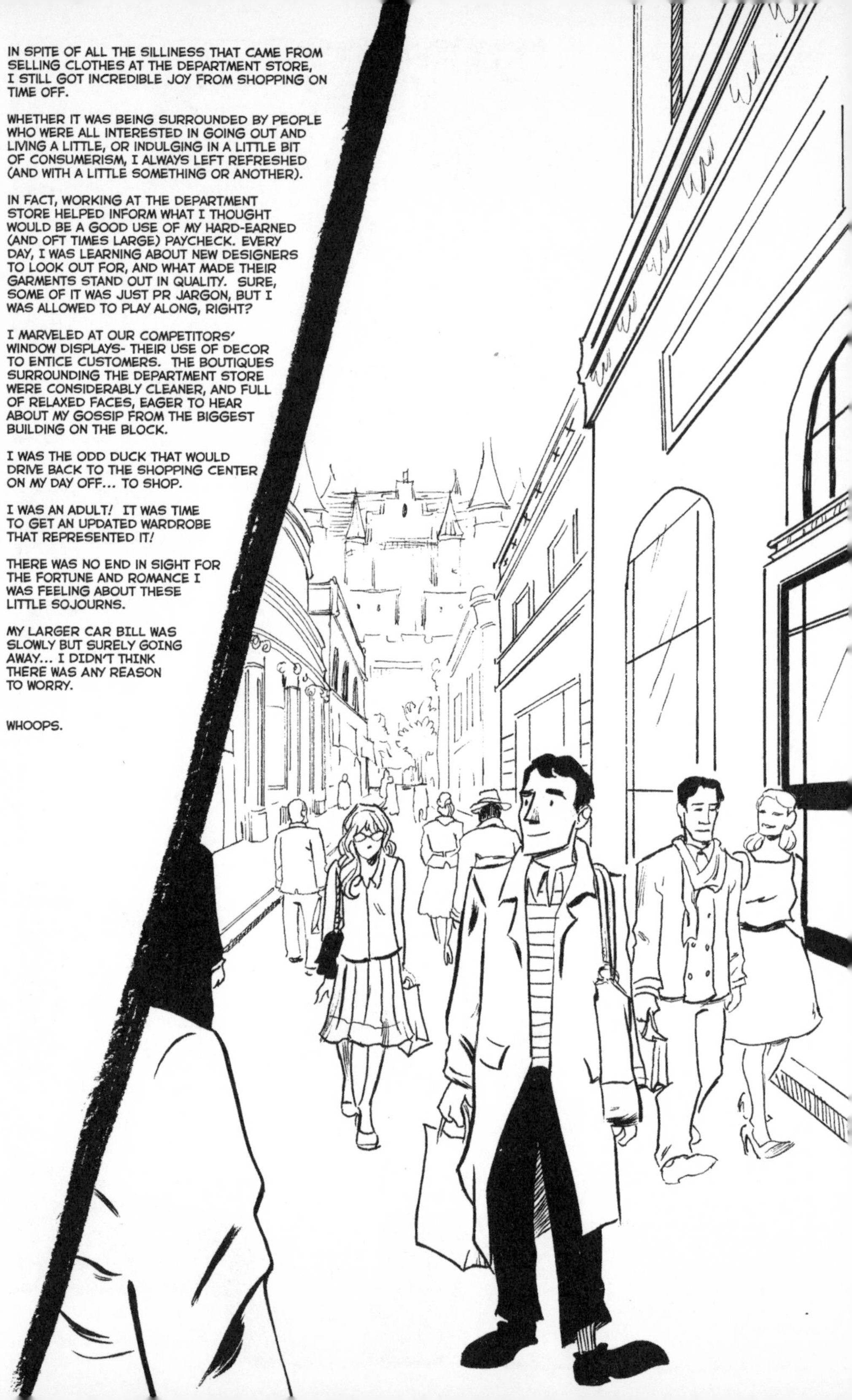
IN SPITE OF ALL THE SILLINESS THAT CAME FROM SELLING CLOTHES AT THE DEPARTMENT STORE, I STILL GOT INCREDIBLE JOY FROM SHOPPING ON TIME OFF.
WHETHER IT WAS BEING SURROUNDED BY PEOPLE WHO WERE ALL INTERESTED IN GOING OUT AND LIVING A LITTLE, OR INDULGING IN A LITTLE BIT OF CONSUMERISM, I ALWAYS LEFT REFRESHED (AND WITH A LITTLE SOMETHING OR ANOTHER).
IN FACT, WORKING AT THE DEPARTMENT STORE HELPED INFORM WHAT I THOUGHT WOULD BE A GOOD USE OF MY HARD-EARNED (AND OFT TIMES LARGE) PAYCHECK. EVERY DAY, I WAS LEARNING ABOUT NEW DESIGNERS TO LOOK OUT FOR, AND WHAT MADE THEIR GARMENTS STAND OUT IN QUALITY. SURE, SOME OF IT WAS JUST PR JARGON, BUT I WAS ALLOWED TO PLAY ALONG, RIGHT?
I MARVELED AT OUR COMPETITORS' WINDOW DISPLAYS- THEIR USE OF DECOR TO ENTICE CUSTOMERS. THE BOUTIQUES SURROUNDING THE DEPARTMENT STORE WERE CONSIDERABLY CLEANER, AND FULL OF RELAXED FACES, EAGER TO HEAR ABOUT MY GOSSIP FROM THE BIGGEST BUILDING ON THE BLOCK.
I WAS THE ODD DUCK THAT WOULD DRIVE BACK TO THE SHOPPING CENTER ON MY DAY OFF... TO SHOP.
I WAS AN ADULT! IT WAS TIME TO GET AN UPDATED WARDROBE THAT REPRESENTED IT!
THERE WAS NO END IN SIGHT FOR THE FORTUNE AND ROMANCE I WAS FEELING ABOUT THESE LITTLE SOJOURNS.
MY LARGER CAR BILL WAS SLOWLY BUT SURELY GOING AWAY... I DIDN'T THINK THERE WAS ANY REASON TO WORRY.
WHOOPS.

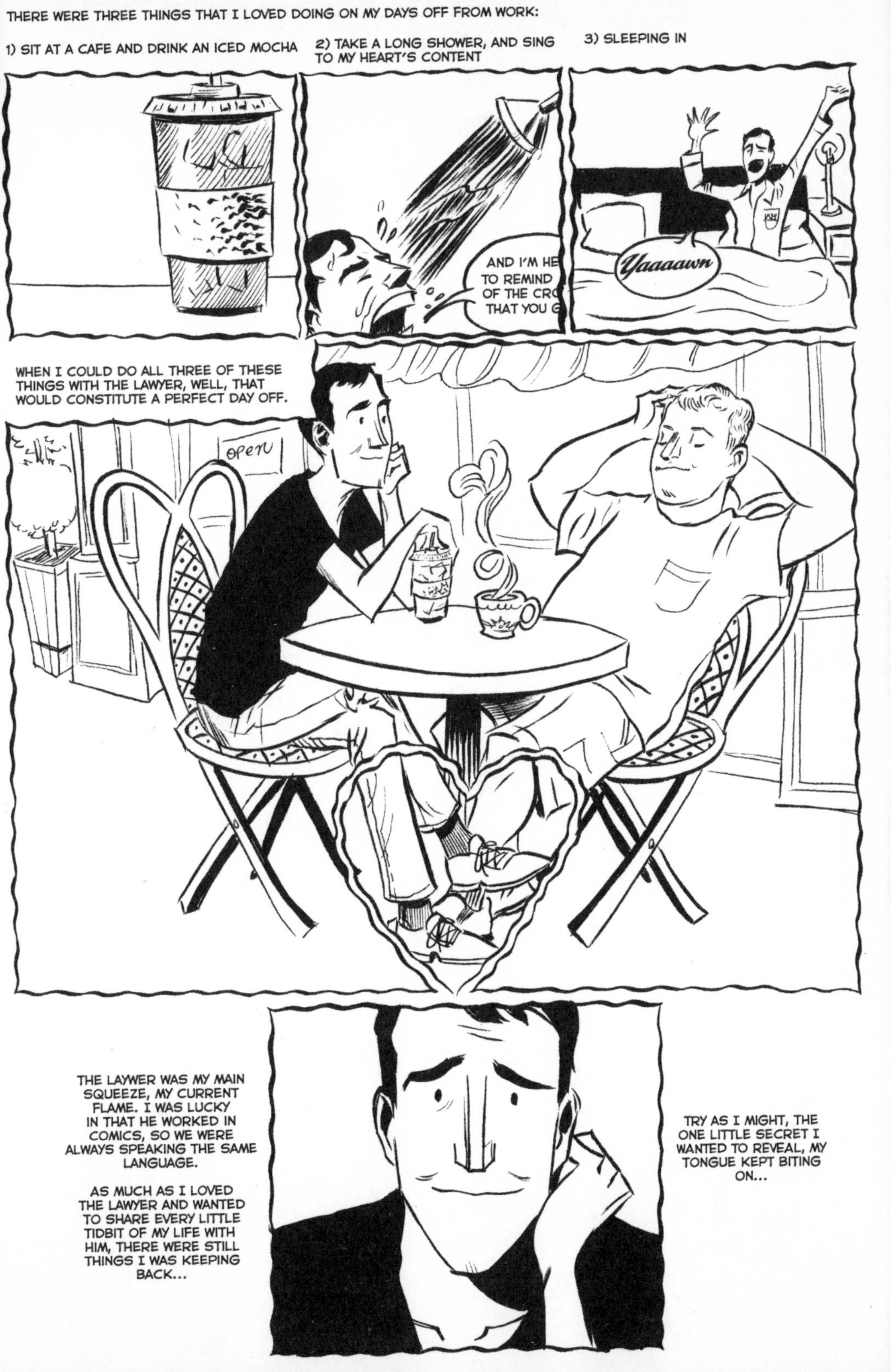
THERE WERE THREE THINGS THAT I LOVED DOING ON MY DAYS OFF FROM WORK:
1) SIT AT A CAFE AND DRINK AN ICED MOCHA
2) TAKE A LONG SHOWER, AND SING TO MY HEART'S CONTENT
3) SLEEPING IN
AND I'M HE TO REMIND OF THE CRO THAT YOU G
Yaaaawn
WHEN I COULD DO ALL THREE OF THESE THINGS WITH THE LAWYER, WELL, THAT WOULD CONSTITUTE A PERFECT DAY OFF.
OPEN
THE LAYWER WAS MY MAIN SQUEEZE, MY CURRENT FLAME. I WAS LUCKY IN THAT HE WORKED IN COMICS, SO WE WERE ALWAYS SPEAKING THE SAME LANGUAGE.
AS MUCH AS I LOVED THE LAWYER AND WANTED TO SHARE EVERY LITTLE TIDBIT OF MY LIFE WITH HIM, THERE WERE STILL THINGS I WAS KEEPING BACK...
TRY AS I MIGHT, THE ONE LITTLE SECRET I WANTED TO REVEAL, MY TONGUE KEPT BITING ON...

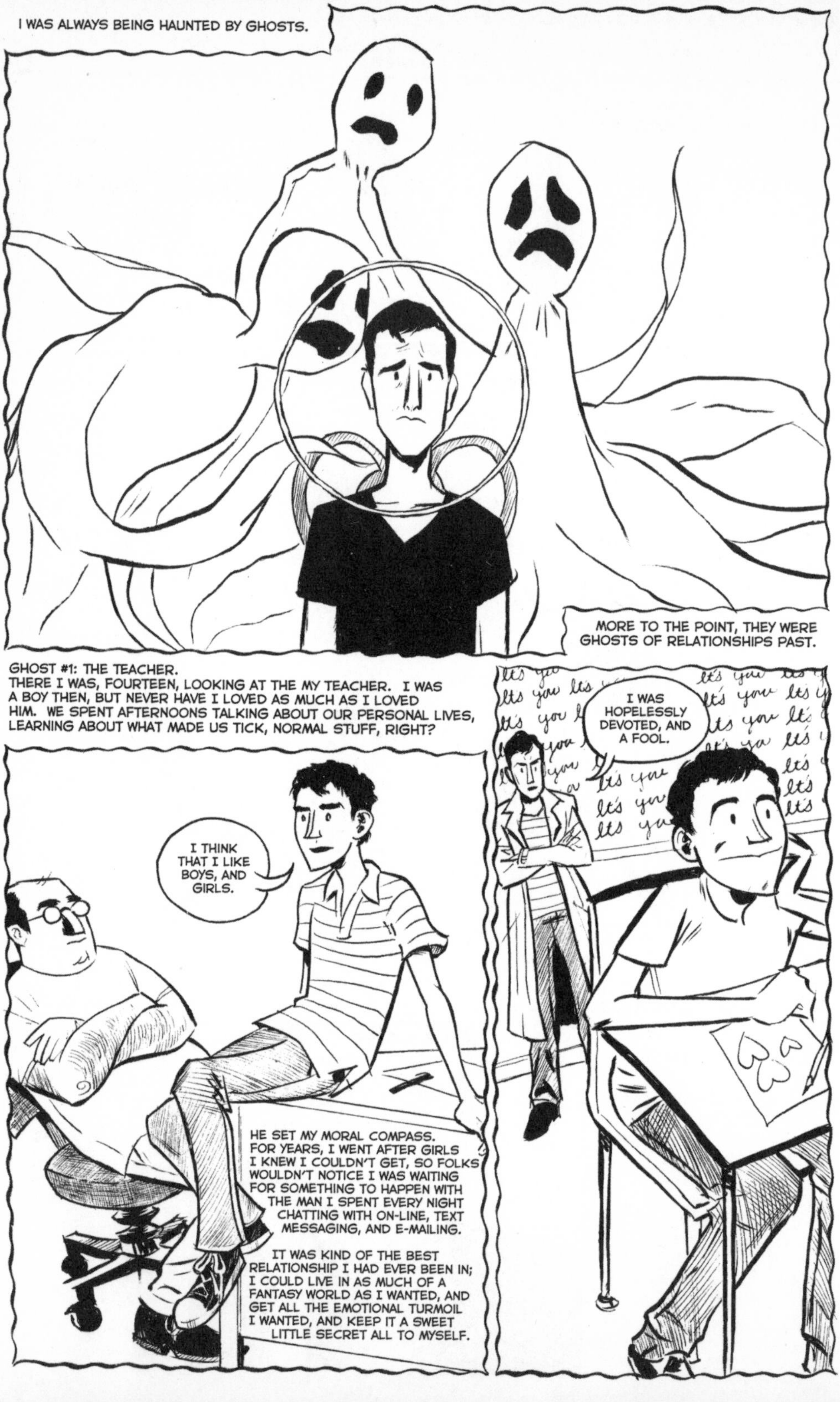
I WAS ALWAYS BEING HAUNTED BY GHOSTS.
MORE TO THE POINT, THEY WERE GHOSTS OF RELATIONSHIPS PAST.
GHOST #1: THE TEACHER.
THERE I WAS, FOURTEEN, LOOKING AT THE MY TEACHER. I WAS A BOY THEN, BUT NEVER HAVE I LOVED AS MUCH AS I LOVED HIM. WE SPENT AFTERNOONS TALKING ABOUT OUR PERSONAL LIVES, LEARNING ABOUT WHAT MADE US TICK, NORMAL STUFF, RIGHT?
I THINK THAT I LIKE BOYS, AND GIRLS.
HE SET MY MORAL COMPASS. FOR YEARS, I WENT AFTER GIRLS I KNEW I COULDN'T GET, SO FOLKS WOULDN'T NOTICE I WAS WAITING FOR SOMETHING TO HAPPEN WITH THE MAN I SPENT EVERY NIGHT CHATTING WITH ON-LINE, TEXT MESSAGING, AND E-MAILING.
IT WAS KIND OF THE BEST RELATIONSHIP I HAD EVER BEEN IN; I COULD LIVE IN AS MUCH OF A FANTASY WORLD AS I WANTED, AND GET ALL THE EMOTIONAL TURMOIL I WANTED, AND KEEP IT A SWEET LITTLE SECRET ALL TO MYSELF.
I WAS HOPELESSLY DEVOTED, AND A FOOL.

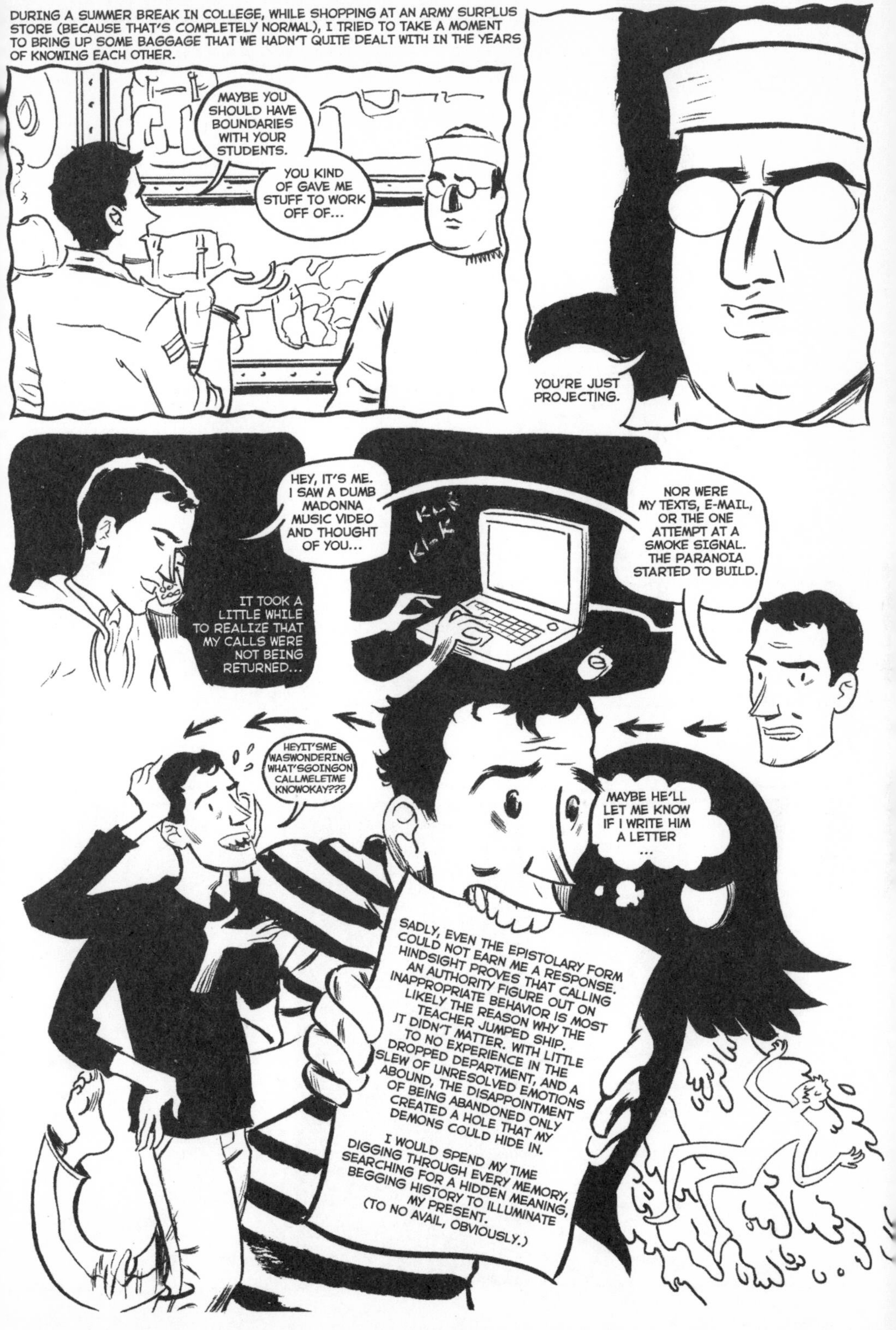
DURING A SUMMER BREAK IN COLLEGE, WHILE SHOPPING AT AN ARMY SURPLUS STORE (BECAUSE THAT'S COMPLETELY NORMAL), I TRIED TO TAKE A MOMENT TO BRING UP SOME BAGGAGE THAT WE HADN'T QUITE DEALT WITH IN THE YEARS OF KNOWING EACH OTHER.
MAYBE YOU SHOULD HAVE BOUNDARIES WITH YOUR STUDENTS.
YOU KIND OF GAVE ME STUFF TO WORK OFF OF...
YOU'RE JUST PROJECTING.
HEY, IT'S ME. I SAW A DUMB MADONNA MUSIC VIDEO AND THOUGHT OF YOU...
KLIK KLIK
IT TOOK A LITTLE WHILE TO REALIZE THAT MY CALLS WERE NOT BEING RETURNED...
NOR WERE MY TEXTS, E-MAIL, OR THE ONE ATTEMPT AT A SMOKE SIGNAL. THE PARANOIA STARTED TO BUILD.
HEYIT'SME WASWONDERING WHAT'SGOINGON CALLMELETME KNOWOKAY???
MAYBE HE'LL LET ME KNOW IF I WRITE HIM A LETTER ...
SADLY, EVEN THE EPISTOLARY FORM COULD NOT EARN ME A RESPONSE. HINDSIGHT PROVES THAT CALLING AN AUTHORITY FIGURE OUT ON INAPPROPRIATE BEHAVIOR IS MOST LIKELY THE REASON WHY THE TEACHER JUMPED SHIP. IT DIDN'T MATTER. WITH LITTLE TO NO EXPERIENCE IN THE DROPPED DEPARTMENT, AND A SLEW OF UNRESOLVED EMOTIONS ABOUND, THE DISAPPOINTMENT OF BEING ABANDONED ONLY CREATED A HOLE THAT MY DEMONS COULD HIDE IN.
I WOULD SPEND MY TIME DIGGING THROUGH EVERY MEMORY, SEARCHING FOR A HIDDEN MEANING, BEGGING HISTORY TO ILLUMINATE MY PRESENT. (TO NO AVAIL, OBVIOUSLY.)

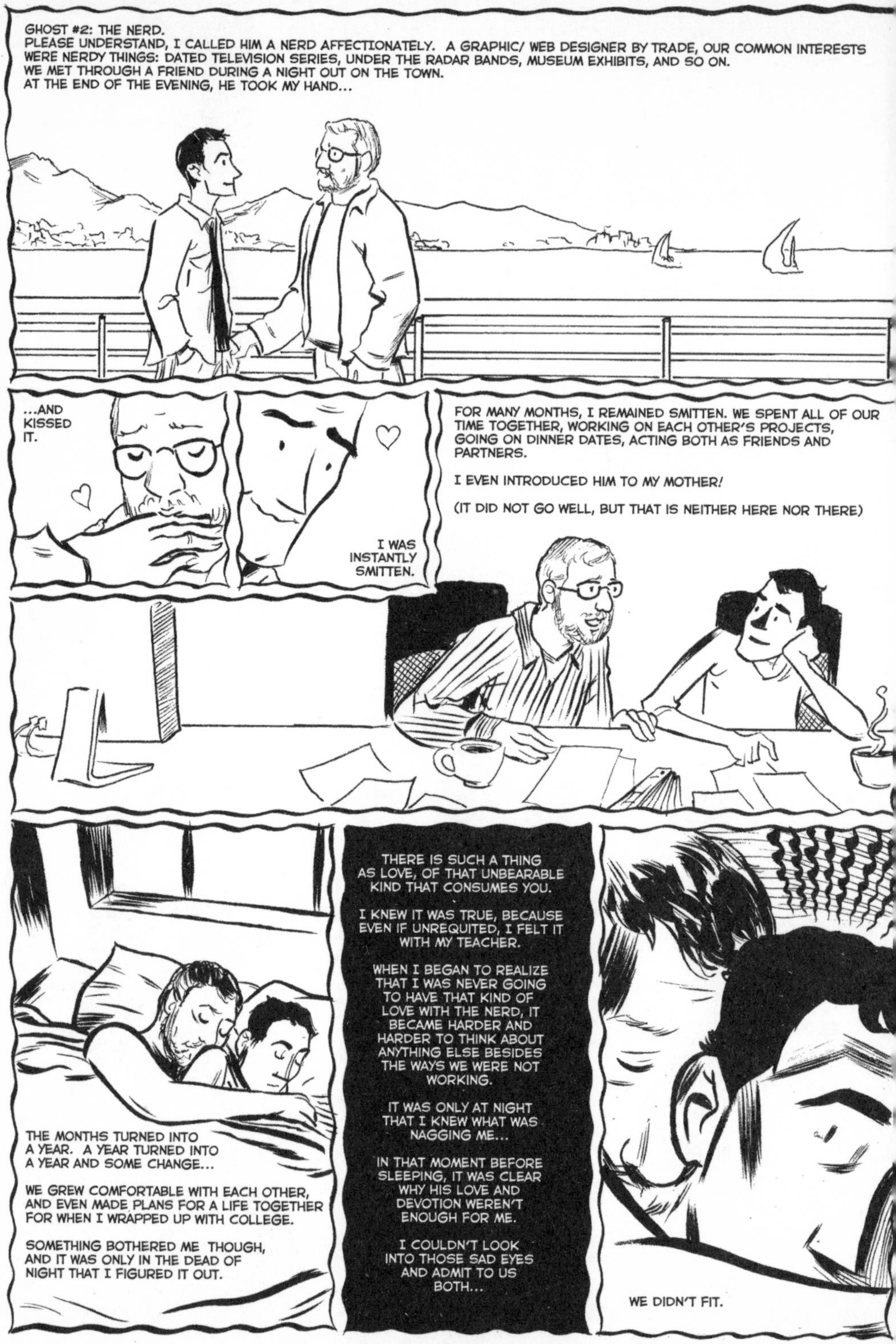
GHOST #2: THE NERD.
PLEASE UNDERSTAND, I CALLED HIM A NERD AFFECTIONATELY. A GRAPHIC/ WEB DESIGNER BY TRADE, OUR COMMON INTERESTS WERE NERDY THINGS: DATED TELEVISION SERIES, UNDER THE RADAR BANDS, MUSEUM EXHIBITS, AND SO ON.
WE MET THROUGH A FRIEND DURING A NIGHT OUT ON THE TOWN.
AT THE END OF THE EVENING, HE TOOK MY HAND...
...AND KISSED IT.
I WAS INSTANTLY SMITTEN.
FOR MANY MONTHS, I REMAINED SMITTEN. WE SPENT ALL OF OUR TIME TOGETHER, WORKING ON EACH OTHER'S PROJECTS, GOING ON DINNER DATES, ACTING BOTH AS FRIENDS AND PARTNERS.
I EVEN INTRODUCED HIM TO MY MOTHER!
(IT DID NOT GO WELL, BUT THAT IS NEITHER HERE NOR THERE)
THE MONTHS TURNED INTO A YEAR. A YEAR TURNED INTO A YEAR AND SOME CHANGE...
WE GREW COMFORTABLE WITH EACH OTHER, AND EVEN MADE PLANS FOR A LIFE TOGETHER FOR WHEN I WRAPPED UP WITH COLLEGE.
SOMETHING BOTHERED ME THOUGH, AND IT WAS ONLY IN THE DEAD OF NIGHT THAT I FIGURED IT OUT.
THERE IS SUCH A THING AS LOVE, OF THAT UNBEARABLE KIND THAT CONSUMES YOU.
I KNEW IT WAS TRUE, BECAUSE EVEN IF UNREQUITED, I FELT IT WITH MY TEACHER.
WHEN I BEGAN TO REALIZE THAT I WAS NEVER GOING TO HAVE THAT KIND OF LOVE WITH THE NERD, IT BECAME HARDER AND HARDER TO THINK ABOUT ANYTHING ELSE BESIDES THE WAYS WE WERE NOT WORKING.
IT WAS ONLY AT NIGHT THAT I KNEW WHAT WAS NAGGING ME...
IN THAT MOMENT BEFORE SLEEPING, IT WAS CLEAR WHY HIS LOVE AND DEVOTION WEREN'T ENOUGH FOR ME.
I COULDN'T LOOK INTO THOSE SAD EYES AND ADMIT TO US BOTH...
WE DIDN'T FIT.

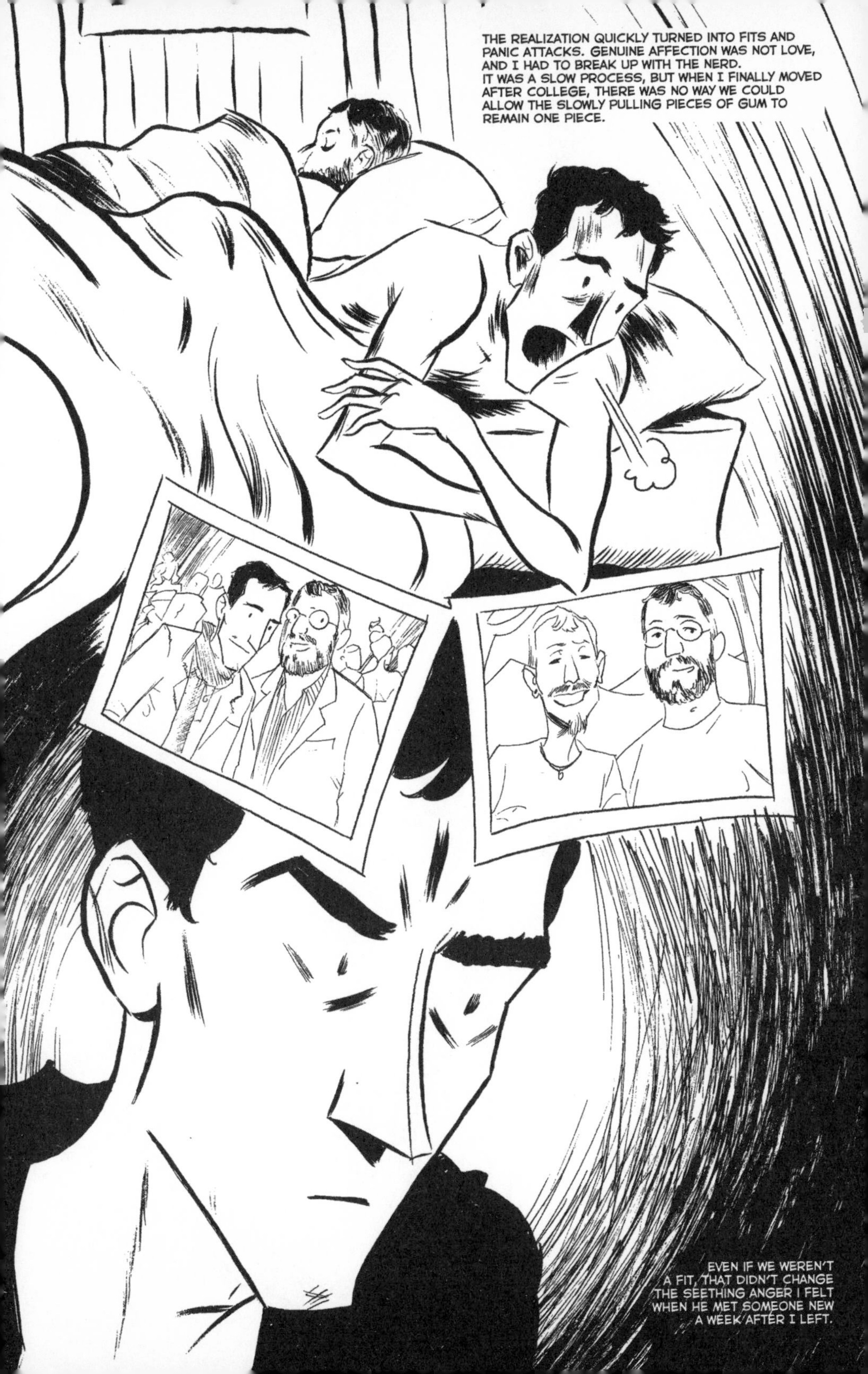
THE REALIZATION QUICKLY TURNED INTO FITS AND PANIC ATTACKS. GENUINE AFFECTION WAS NOT LOVE, AND I HAD TO BREAK UP WITH THE NERD.
IT WAS A SLOW PROCESS, BUT WHEN I FINALLY MOVED AFTER COLLEGE, THERE WAS NO WAY WE COULD ALLOW THE SLOWLY PULLING PIECES OF GUM TO REMAIN ONE PIECE.
EVEN IF WE WEREN'T A FIT, THAT DIDN'T CHANGE THE SEETHING ANGER I FELT WHEN HE MET SOMEONE NEW A WEEK AFTER I LEFT.

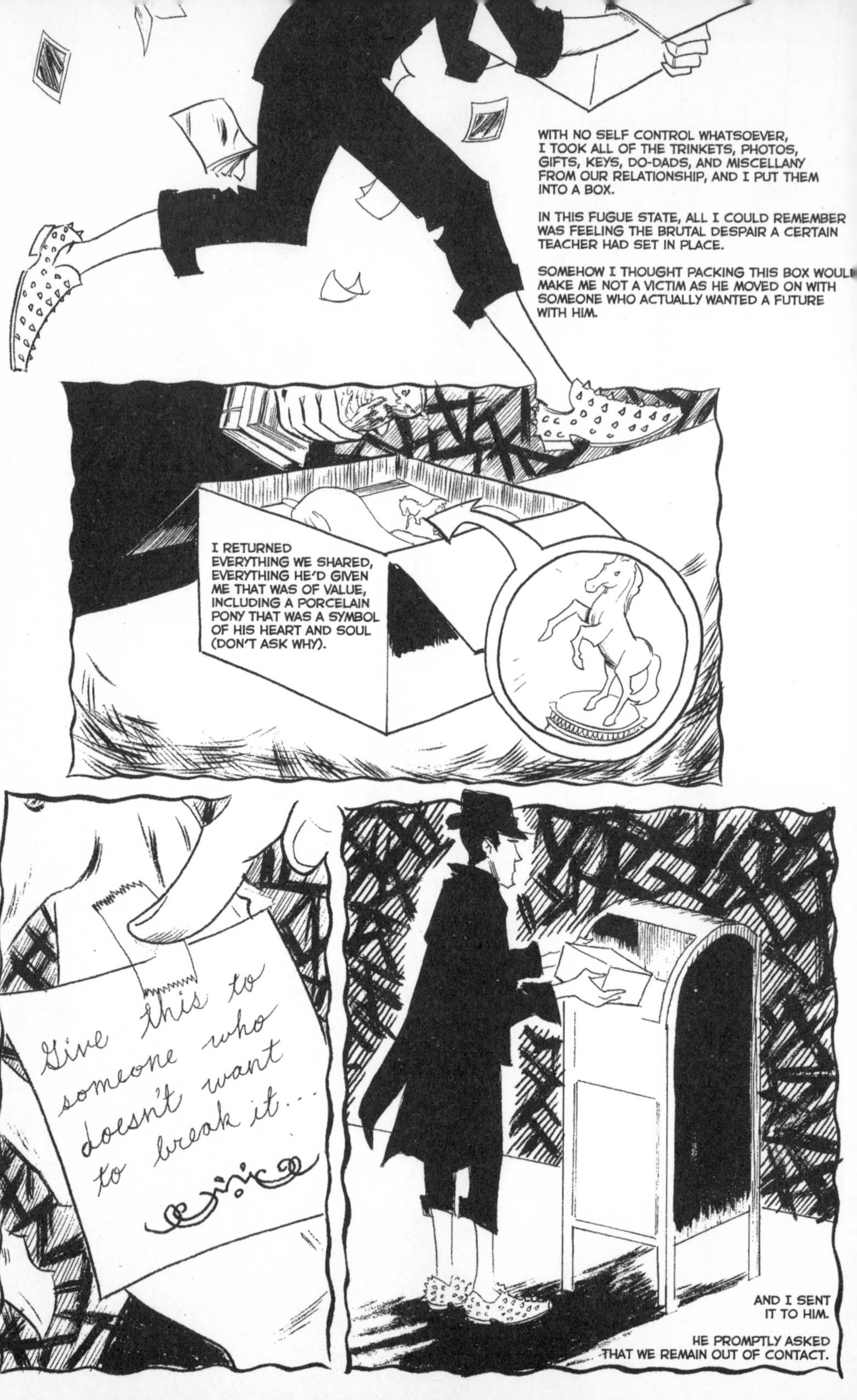
WITH NO SELF CONTROL WHATSOEVER, I TOOK ALL OF THE TRINKETS, PHOTOS, GIFTS, KEYS, DO-DADS, AND MISCELLANY FROM OUR RELATIONSHIP, AND I PUT THEM INTO A BOX.
IN THIS FUGUE STATE, ALL I COULD REMEMBER WAS FEELING THE BRUTAL DESPAIR A CERTAIN TEACHER HAD SET IN PLACE.
SOMEHOW I THOUGHT PACKING THIS BOX WOULD MAKE ME NOT A VICTIM AS HE MOVED ON WITH SOMEONE WHO ACTUALLY WANTED A FUTURE WITH HIM.
I RETURNED EVERYTHING WE SHARED, EVERYTHING HE'D GIVEN ME THAT WAS OF VALUE, INCLUDING A PORCELAIN PONY THAT WAS A SYMBOL OF HIS HEART AND SOUL (DON'T ASK WHY).
Give this to someone who doesn't want to break it...
AND I SENT IT TO HIM.
HE PROMPTLY ASKED THAT WE REMAIN OUT OF CONTACT.

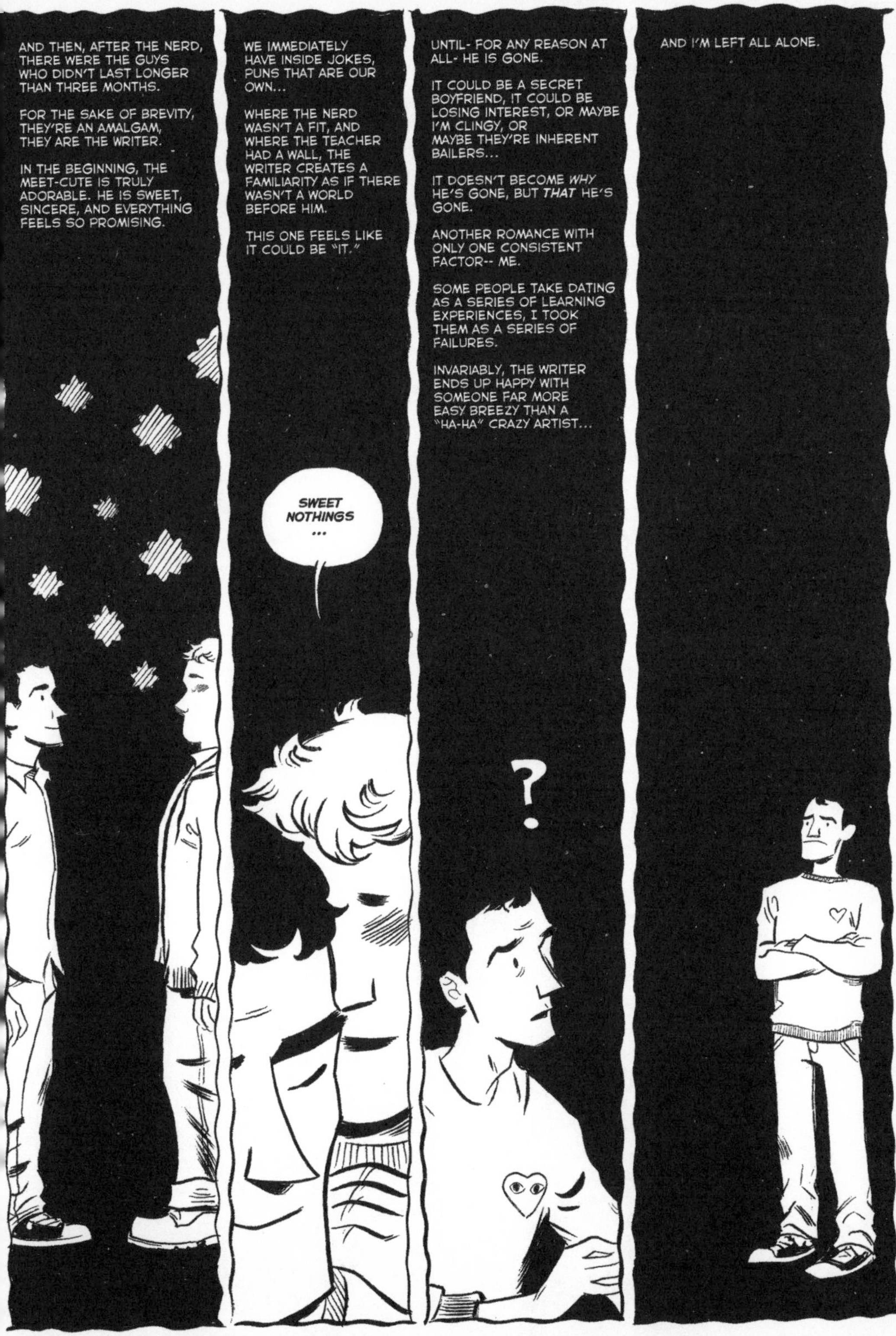
AND THEN, AFTER THE NERD, THERE WERE THE GUYS WHO DIDN'T LAST LONGER THAN THREE MONTHS.
FOR THE SAKE OF BREVITY, THEY'RE AN AMALGAM, THEY ARE THE WRITER.
IN THE BEGINNING, THE MEET-CUTE IS TRULY ADORABLE. HE IS SWEET, SINCERE, AND EVERYTHING FEELS SO PROMISING.
WE IMMEDIATELY HAVE INSIDE JOKES, PUNS THAT ARE OUR OWN...
WHERE THE NERD WASN'T A FIT, AND WHERE THE TEACHER HAD A WALL, THE WRITER CREATES A FAMILIARITY AS IF THERE WASN'T A WORLD BEFORE HIM.
THIS ONE FEELS LIKE IT COULD BE "IT."
SWEET NOTHINGS ...
UNTIL- FOR ANY REASON AT ALL- HE IS GONE.
IT COULD BE A SECRET BOYFRIEND, IT COULD BE LOSING INTEREST, OR MAYBE I'M CLINGY, OR MAYBE THEY'RE INHERENT BAILERS...
IT DOESN'T BECOME *WHY* HE'S GONE, BUT *THAT* HE'S GONE.
ANOTHER ROMANCE WITH ONLY ONE CONSISTENT FACTOR-- ME.
SOME PEOPLE TAKE DATING AS A SERIES OF LEARNING EXPERIENCES, I TOOK THEM AS A SERIES OF FAILURES.
INVARIABLY, THE WRITER ENDS UP HAPPY WITH SOMEONE FAR MORE EASY BREEZY THAN A "HA-HA" CRAZY ARTIST...
?
AND I'M LEFT ALL ALONE.

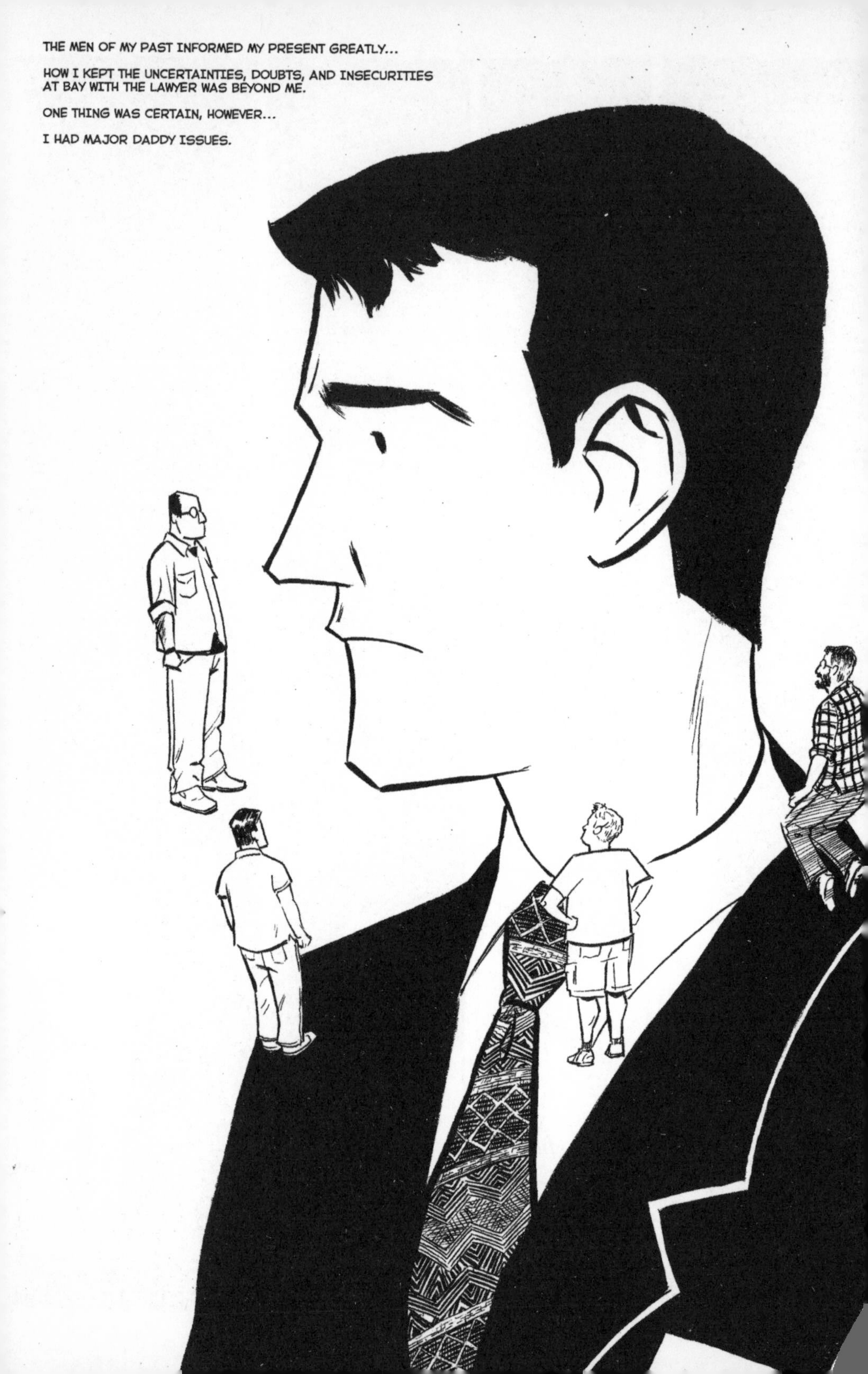
THE MEN OF MY PAST INFORMED MY PRESENT GREATLY...
HOW I KEPT THE UNCERTAINTIES, DOUBTS, AND INSECURITIES AT BAY WITH THE LAWYER WAS BEYOND ME.
ONE THING WAS CERTAIN, HOWEVER...
I HAD MAJOR DADDY ISSUES.

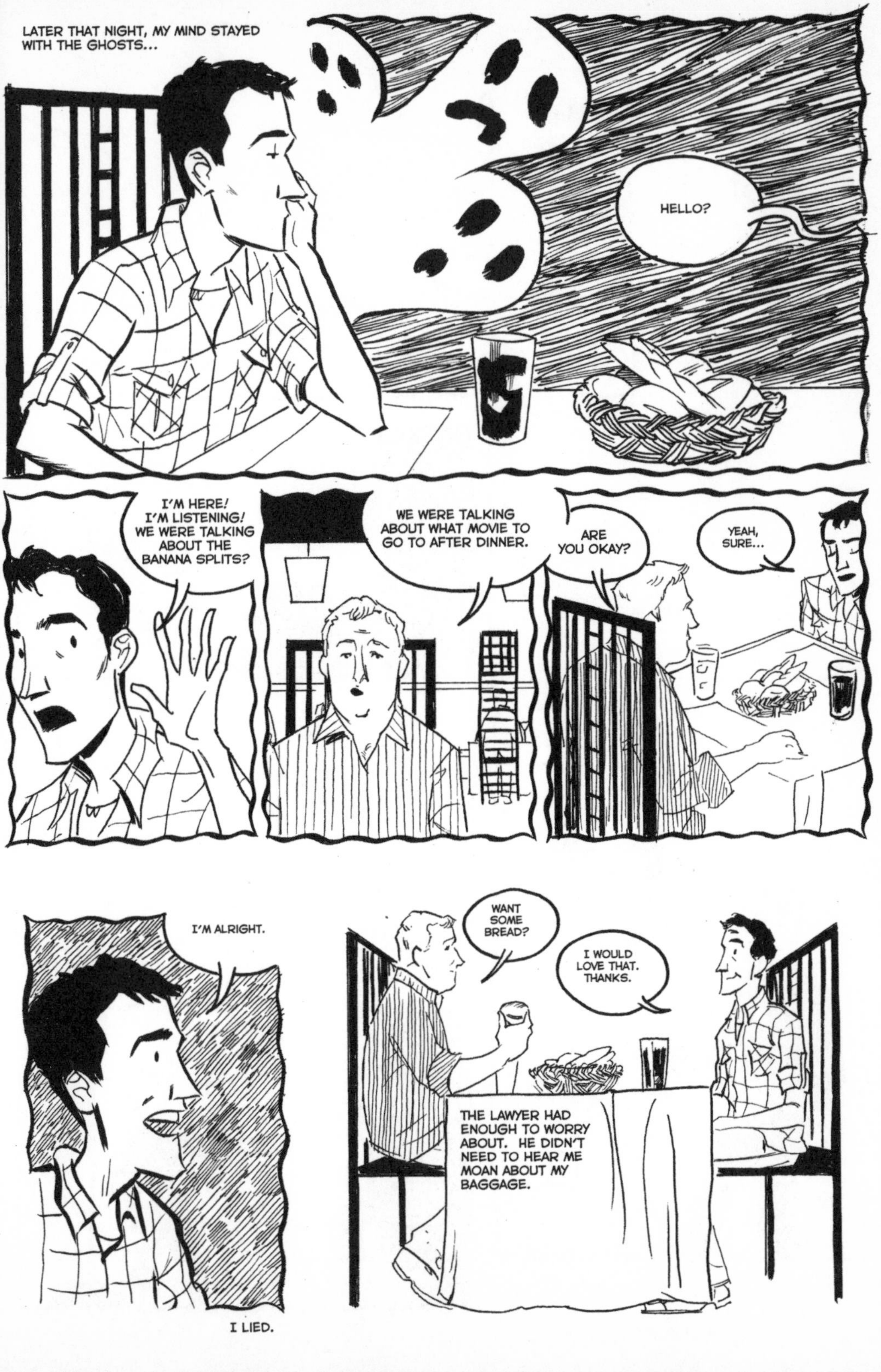
LATER THAT NIGHT, MY MIND STAYED WITH THE GHOSTS...
HELLO?
I'M HERE! I'M LISTENING! WE WERE TALKING ABOUT THE BANANA SPLITS?
WE WERE TALKING ABOUT WHAT MOVIE TO GO TO AFTER DINNER.
ARE YOU OKAY?
YEAH, SURE...
I'M ALRIGHT.
I LIED.
WANT SOME BREAD?
I WOULD LOVE THAT. THANKS.
THE LAWYER HAD ENOUGH TO WORRY ABOUT. HE DIDN'T NEED TO HEAR ME MOAN ABOUT MY BAGGAGE.

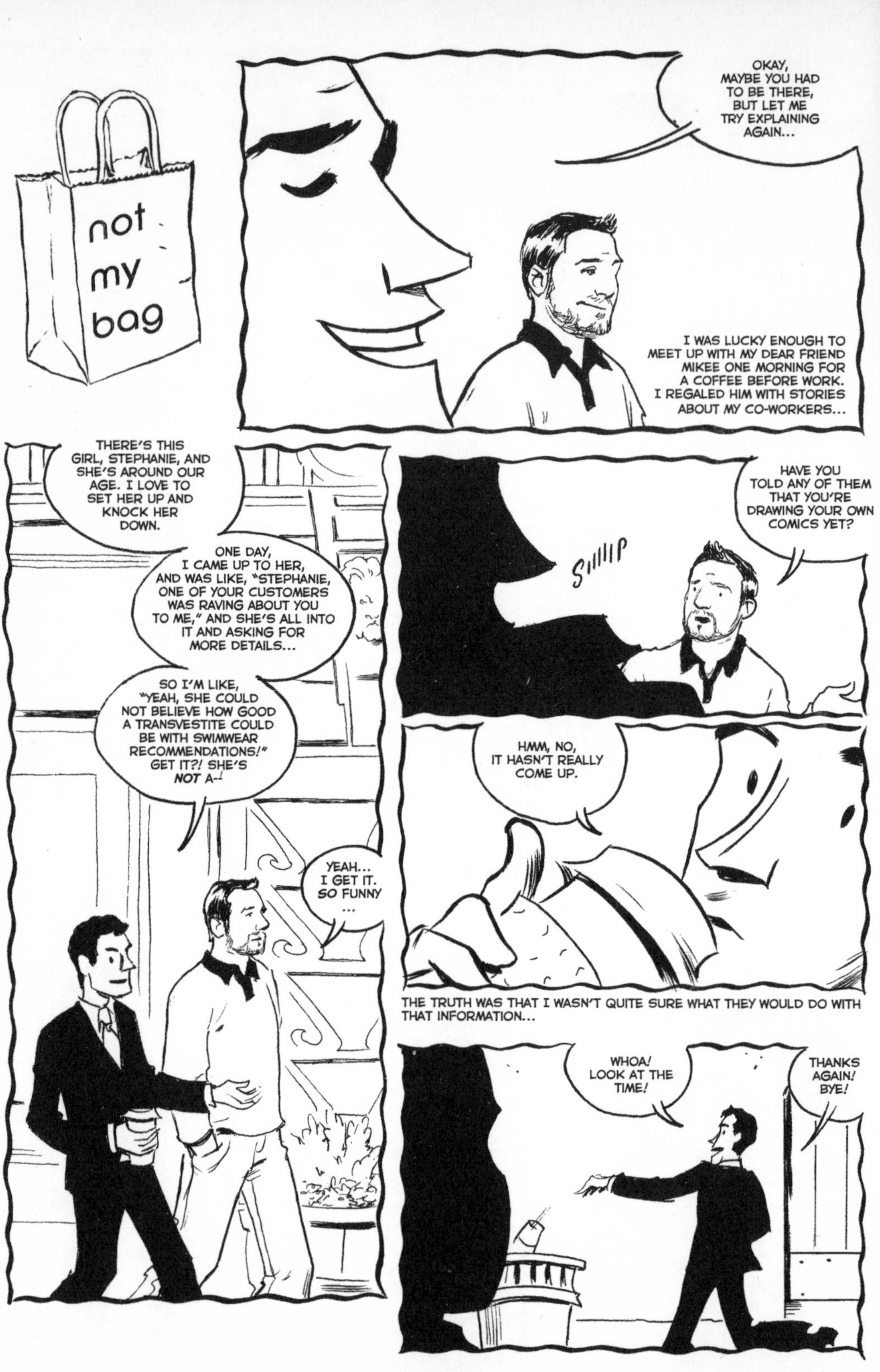
not my bag
OKAY, MAYBE YOU HAD TO BE THERE, BUT LET ME TRY EXPLAINING AGAIN...
I WAS LUCKY ENOUGH TO MEET UP WITH MY DEAR FRIEND MIKEE ONE MORNING FOR A COFFEE BEFORE WORK. I REGALED HIM WITH STORIES ABOUT MY CO-WORKERS...
THERE'S THIS GIRL, STEPHANIE, AND SHE'S AROUND OUR AGE. I LOVE TO SET HER UP AND KNOCK HER DOWN.
ONE DAY, I CAME UP TO HER, AND WAS LIKE, "STEPHANIE, ONE OF YOUR CUSTOMERS WAS RAVING ABOUT YOU TO ME," AND SHE'S ALL INTO IT AND ASKING FOR MORE DETAILS...
SO I'M LIKE, "YEAH, SHE COULD NOT BELIEVE HOW GOOD A TRANSVESTITE COULD BE WITH SWIMWEAR RECOMMENDATIONS!" GET IT?! SHE'S *NOT* A--
YEAH... I GET IT. *SO* FUNNY ...
SIIIIP
HAVE YOU TOLD ANY OF THEM THAT YOU'RE DRAWING YOUR OWN COMICS YET?
HMM, NO, IT HASN'T REALLY COME UP.
THE TRUTH WAS THAT I WASN'T QUITE SURE WHAT THEY WOULD DO WITH THAT INFORMATION...
WHOA! LOOK AT THE TIME!
THANKS AGAIN! BYE!

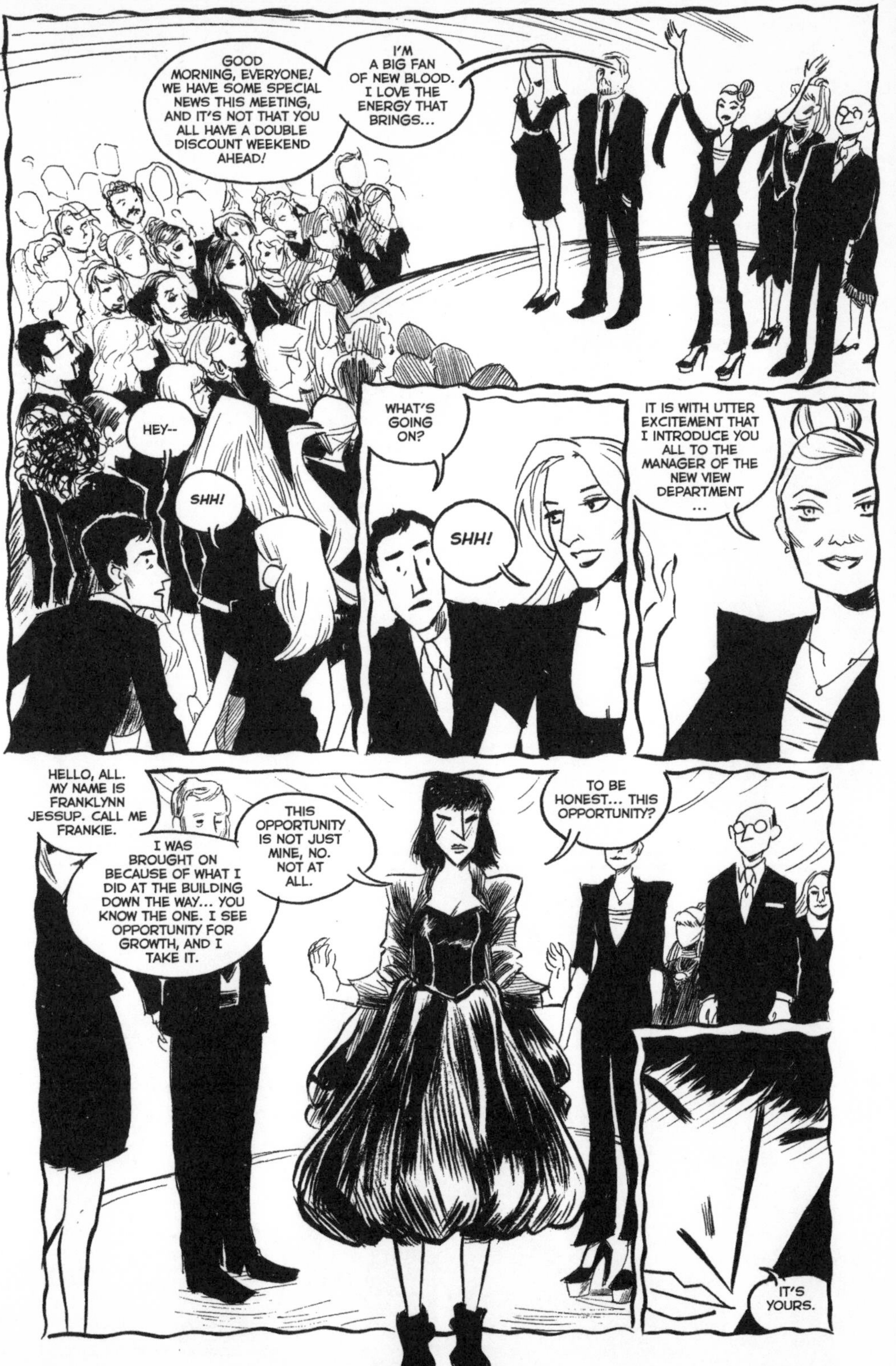
GOOD MORNING, EVERYONE! WE HAVE SOME SPECIAL NEWS THIS MEETING, AND IT'S NOT THAT YOU ALL HAVE A DOUBLE DISCOUNT WEEKEND AHEAD!
I'M A BIG FAN OF NEW BLOOD. I LOVE THE ENERGY THAT BRINGS...
HEY--
SHH!
WHAT'S GOING ON?
SHH!
IT IS WITH UTTER EXCITEMENT THAT I INTRODUCE YOU ALL TO THE MANAGER OF THE NEW VIEW DEPARTMENT ...
HELLO, ALL. MY NAME IS FRANKLYNN JESSUP. CALL ME FRANKIE.
I WAS BROUGHT ON BECAUSE OF WHAT I DID AT THE BUILDING DOWN THE WAY... YOU KNOW THE ONE. I SEE OPPORTUNITY FOR GROWTH, AND I TAKE IT.
THIS OPPORTUNITY IS NOT JUST MINE, NO. NOT AT ALL.
TO BE HONEST... THIS OPPORTUNITY?
IT'S YOURS.

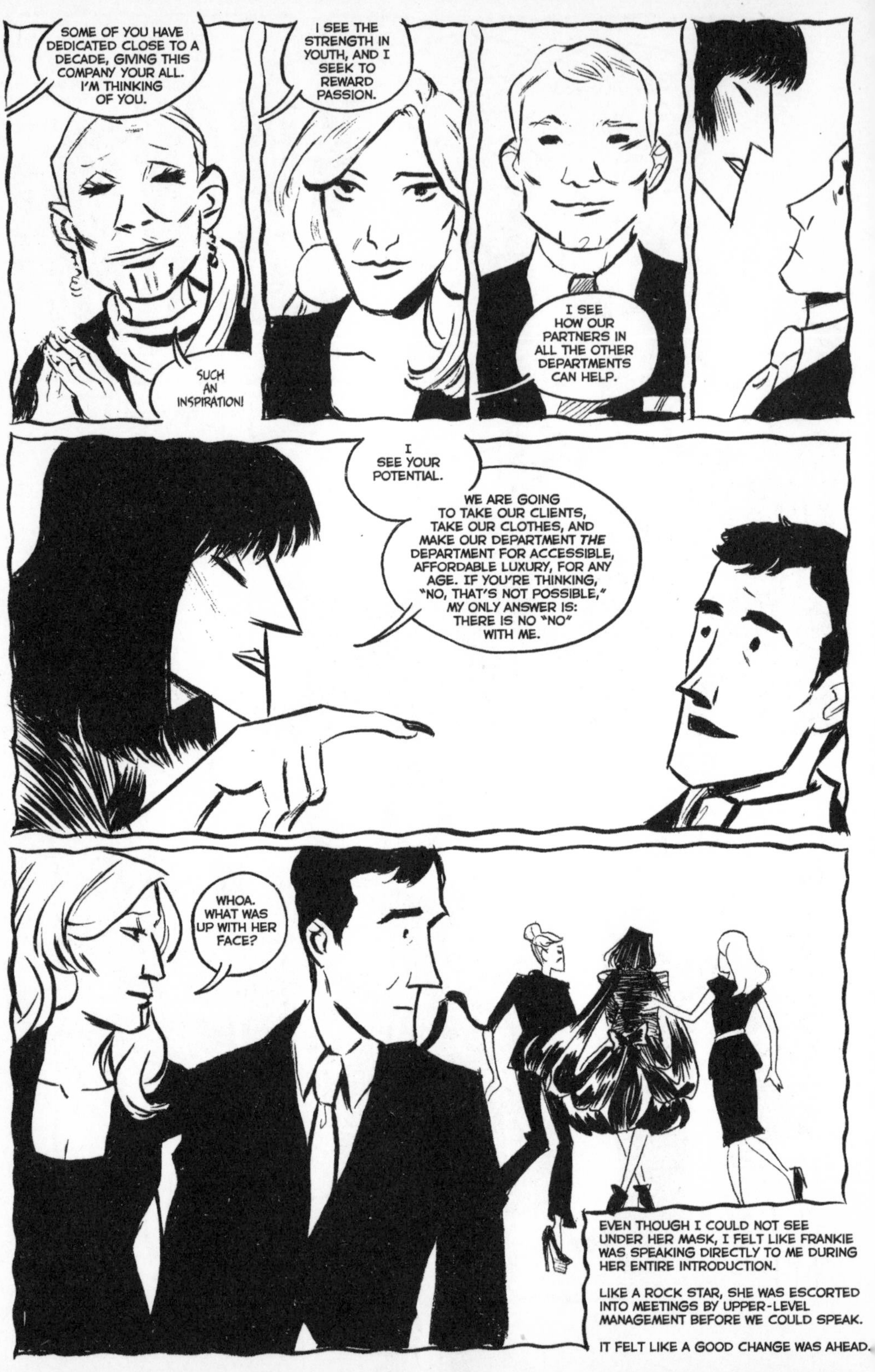
SOME OF YOU HAVE DEDICATED CLOSE TO A DECADE, GIVING THIS COMPANY YOUR ALL. I'M THINKING OF YOU.
SUCH AN INSPIRATION!
I SEE THE STRENGTH IN YOUTH, AND I SEEK TO REWARD PASSION.
I SEE HOW OUR PARTNERS IN ALL THE OTHER DEPARTMENTS CAN HELP.
I SEE YOUR POTENTIAL.
WE ARE GOING TO TAKE OUR CLIENTS, TAKE OUR CLOTHES, AND MAKE OUR DEPARTMENT *THE* DEPARTMENT FOR ACCESSIBLE, AFFORDABLE LUXURY, FOR ANY AGE. IF YOU'RE THINKING, "NO, THAT'S NOT POSSIBLE," MY ONLY ANSWER IS: THERE IS NO "NO" WITH ME.
WHOA. WHAT WAS UP WITH HER FACE?
EVEN THOUGH I COULD NOT SEE UNDER HER MASK, I FELT LIKE FRANKIE WAS SPEAKING DIRECTLY TO ME DURING HER ENTIRE INTRODUCTION.
LIKE A ROCK STAR, SHE WAS ESCORTED INTO MEETINGS BY UPPER-LEVEL MANAGEMENT BEFORE WE COULD SPEAK.
IT FELT LIKE A GOOD CHANGE WAS AHEAD.

chapter
two

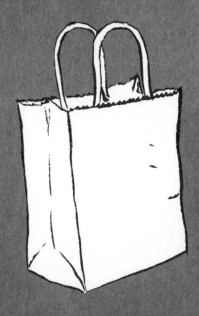

"Behind every great
fortune lies a crime."

--Honore de Balzac

AS I BEGAN TO LEARN MORE ABOUT FASHION, THERE WERE
LINES AND BOUNDARIES I BEGAN CROSSING.
SYMMETRICAL CLOTHING-- BORING!
KNEE-HIGH PURPLE KNIT SOCKS-- A MUST!
LEOPARD PRINT-- BOTH FAUX PAS AND FALL PATTERN!

I WAS LUCKY ENOUGH THAT ALONG THE WAY I HAD FRIENDS
WITH THE DECENCY TO TELL ME WHEN I WAS MAKING ANY
TRULY BAD DECISIONS...

YEAH,
DUDES AREN'T
ALLOWED TO WEAR
CLUTCHES...
EVER.

GIRL,
FASHION IS
SUPPOSED TO
BE PAINFUL, NOT
ITCHY!

IT WAS ALL IN THE GOOD
NAME OF RESEARCH!
I WAS ON THE HUNT FOR
PERFECT WORK
ACCESSORIES...

BEHOLD! MY MOST COVETED PIECES THAT SPRUCED
UP A PLAIN BLACK SUIT, OR POPPED OUT FROM MY
GREY VEST AND PANTS.
WHO KNEW THAT A HOLLOWED OUT ANTLER COULD
MAKE A DIVINE RING (AND THAT I'D FIND IT IN SAN
DIEGO)?

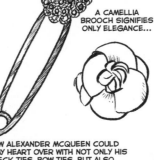

A CAMELLIA
BROOCH SIGNIFIES
ONLY ELEGANCE...

HOW ALEXANDER MCQUEEN COULD
WIN MY HEART OVER WITH NOT ONLY HIS
NECK TIES, BOW TIES, BUT ALSO
HAT PINS (WHICH I STUCK ON MY
LAPEL) IS BEYOND ME!
EVERY PIECE I HAD SEEMED TO
ALWAYS GUARANTEE A COMPLIMENT
FROM THE CUSTOMERS, AND AN ENVIOUS
GLARE FROM MY CO-WORKERS...

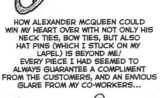

PAUL SMITH=
AMAZING CUFF LINKS

A YSL
CLUSTER
OF CHAINS AND
SAFETY PINS CAN
FIX ANY DULL
CARDIGAN!

OF COURSE, THERE STILL MANAGED TO BE A
FEW FASHION FAILS...

FAGGOT.

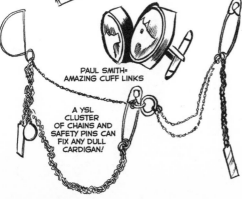

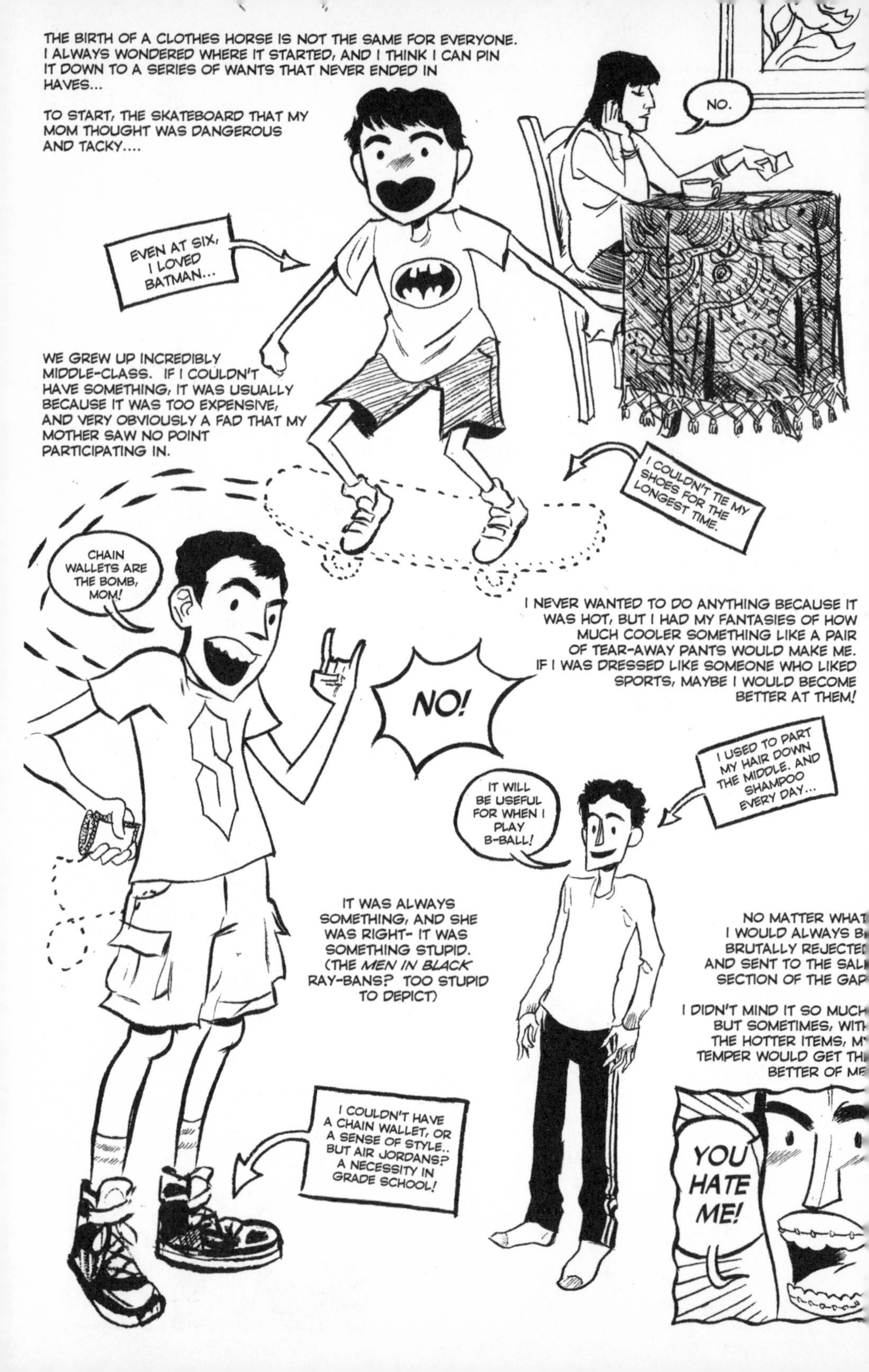
THE BIRTH OF A CLOTHES HORSE IS NOT THE SAME FOR EVERYONE. I ALWAYS WONDERED WHERE IT STARTED, AND I THINK I CAN PIN IT DOWN TO A SERIES OF WANTS THAT NEVER ENDED IN HAVES...
TO START, THE SKATEBOARD THAT MY MOM THOUGHT WAS DANGEROUS AND TACKY....
NO.
EVEN AT SIX, I LOVED BATMAN...
WE GREW UP INCREDIBLY MIDDLE-CLASS. IF I COULDN'T HAVE SOMETHING, IT WAS USUALLY BECAUSE IT WAS TOO EXPENSIVE, AND VERY OBVIOUSLY A FAD THAT MY MOTHER SAW NO POINT PARTICIPATING IN.
I COULDN'T TIE MY SHOES FOR THE LONGEST TIME.
CHAIN WALLETS ARE THE BOMB, MOM!
NO!
I NEVER WANTED TO DO ANYTHING BECAUSE IT WAS HOT, BUT I HAD MY FANTASIES OF HOW MUCH COOLER SOMETHING LIKE A PAIR OF TEAR-AWAY PANTS WOULD MAKE ME. IF I WAS DRESSED LIKE SOMEONE WHO LIKED SPORTS, MAYBE I WOULD BECOME BETTER AT THEM!
IT WILL BE USEFUL FOR WHEN I PLAY B-BALL!
I USED TO PART MY HAIR DOWN THE MIDDLE. AND SHAMPOO EVERY DAY...
IT WAS ALWAYS SOMETHING, AND SHE WAS RIGHT- IT WAS SOMETHING STUPID. (THE *MEN IN BLACK* RAY-BANS? TOO STUPID TO DEPICT)
NO MATTER WHAT I WOULD ALWAYS B BRUTALLY REJECTE AND SENT TO THE SAL SECTION OF THE GAP
I DIDN'T MIND IT SO MUCH BUT SOMETIMES, WIT THE HOTTER ITEMS, M TEMPER WOULD GET TH BETTER OF M
I COULDN'T HAVE A CHAIN WALLET, OR A SENSE OF STYLE.. BUT AIR JORDANS? A NECESSITY IN GRADE SCHOOL!
YOU HATE ME!

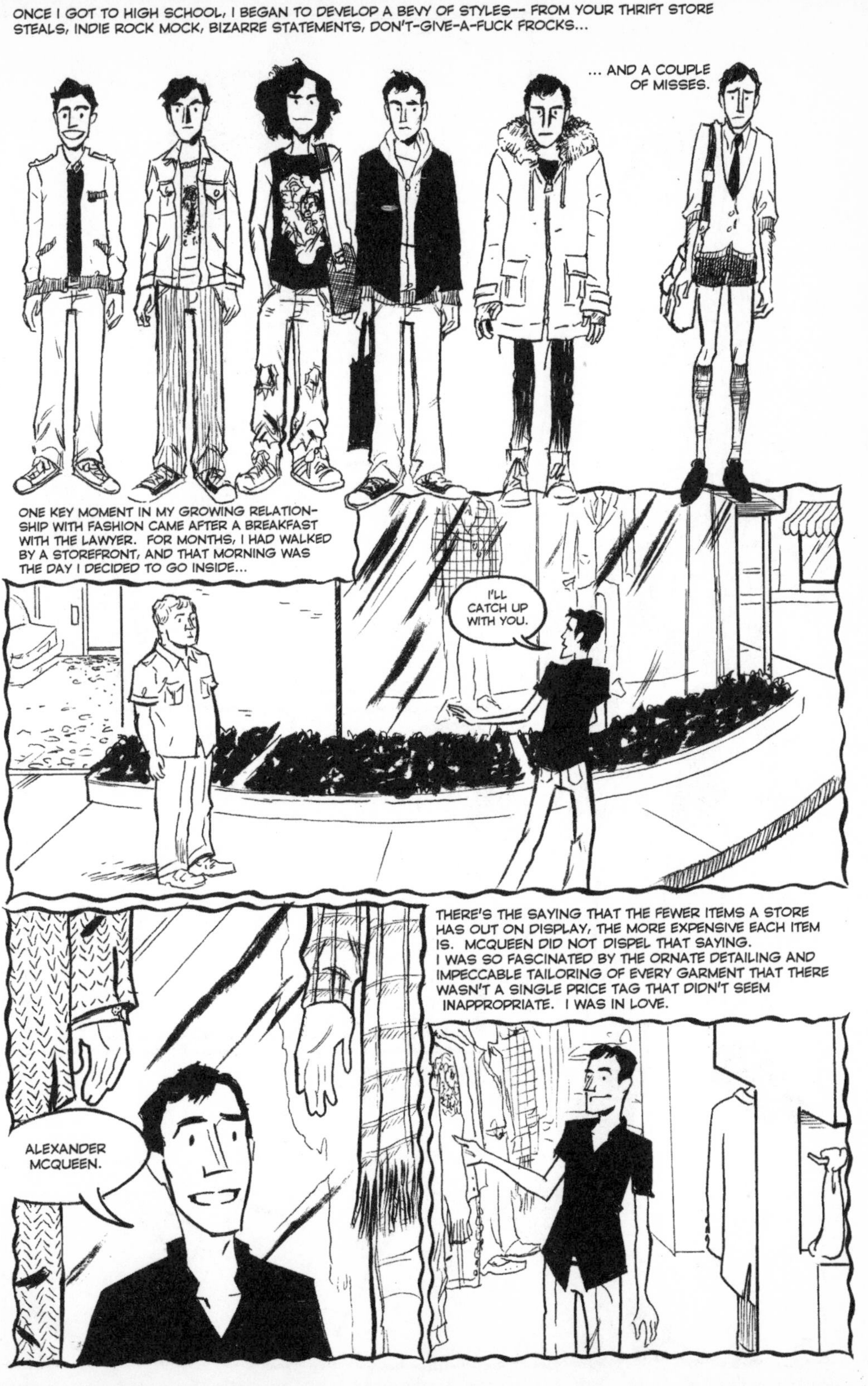
ONCE I GOT TO HIGH SCHOOL, I BEGAN TO DEVELOP A BEVY OF STYLES-- FROM YOUR THRIFT STORE STEALS, INDIE ROCK MOCK, BIZARRE STATEMENTS, DON'T-GIVE-A-FUCK FROCKS...
... AND A COUPLE OF MISSES.
ONE KEY MOMENT IN MY GROWING RELATIONSHIP WITH FASHION CAME AFTER A BREAKFAST WITH THE LAWYER. FOR MONTHS, I HAD WALKED BY A STOREFRONT, AND THAT MORNING WAS THE DAY I DECIDED TO GO INSIDE...
I'LL CATCH UP WITH YOU.
ALEXANDER MCQUEEN.
THERE'S THE SAYING THAT THE FEWER ITEMS A STORE HAS OUT ON DISPLAY, THE MORE EXPENSIVE EACH ITEM IS. MCQUEEN DID NOT DISPEL THAT SAYING. I WAS SO FASCINATED BY THE ORNATE DETAILING AND IMPECCABLE TAILORING OF EVERY GARMENT THAT THERE WASN'T A SINGLE PRICE TAG THAT DIDN'T SEEM INAPPROPRIATE. I WAS IN LOVE.

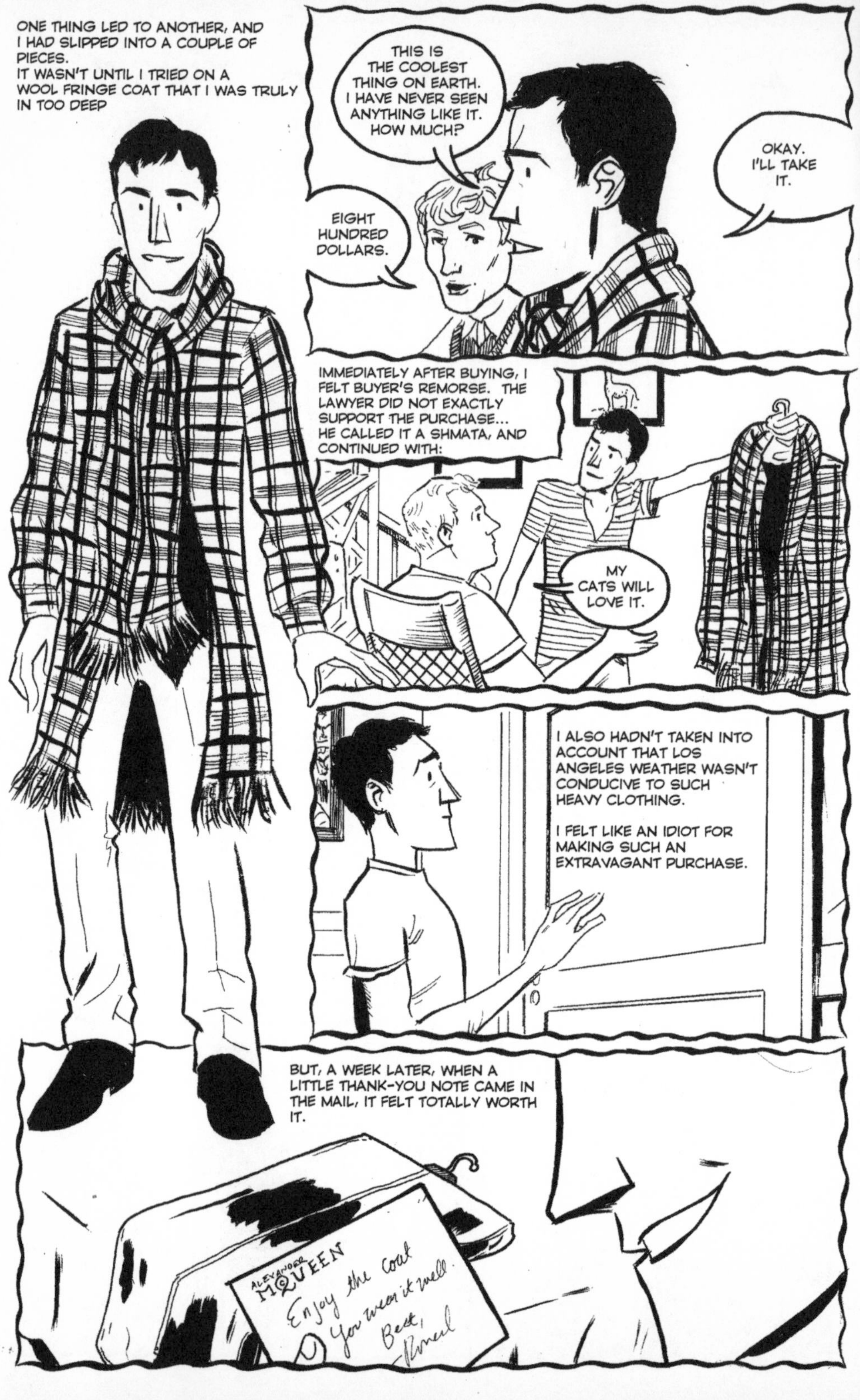
ONE THING LED TO ANOTHER, AND I HAD SLIPPED INTO A COUPLE OF PIECES.
IT WASN'T UNTIL I TRIED ON A WOOL FRINGE COAT THAT I WAS TRULY IN TOO DEEP
THIS IS THE COOLEST THING ON EARTH. I HAVE NEVER SEEN ANYTHING LIKE IT. HOW MUCH?
EIGHT HUNDRED DOLLARS.
OKAY. I'LL TAKE IT.
IMMEDIATELY AFTER BUYING, I FELT BUYER'S REMORSE. THE LAWYER DID NOT EXACTLY SUPPORT THE PURCHASE... HE CALLED IT A SHMATA, AND CONTINUED WITH:
MY CATS WILL LOVE IT.
I ALSO HADN'T TAKEN INTO ACCOUNT THAT LOS ANGELES WEATHER WASN'T CONDUCIVE TO SUCH HEAVY CLOTHING.
I FELT LIKE AN IDIOT FOR MAKING SUCH AN EXTRAVAGANT PURCHASE.
BUT, A WEEK LATER, WHEN A LITTLE THANK-YOU NOTE CAME IN THE MAIL, IT FELT TOTALLY WORTH IT.
ALEXANDER MCQUEEN
Enjoy the coat
You wear it well
Best,

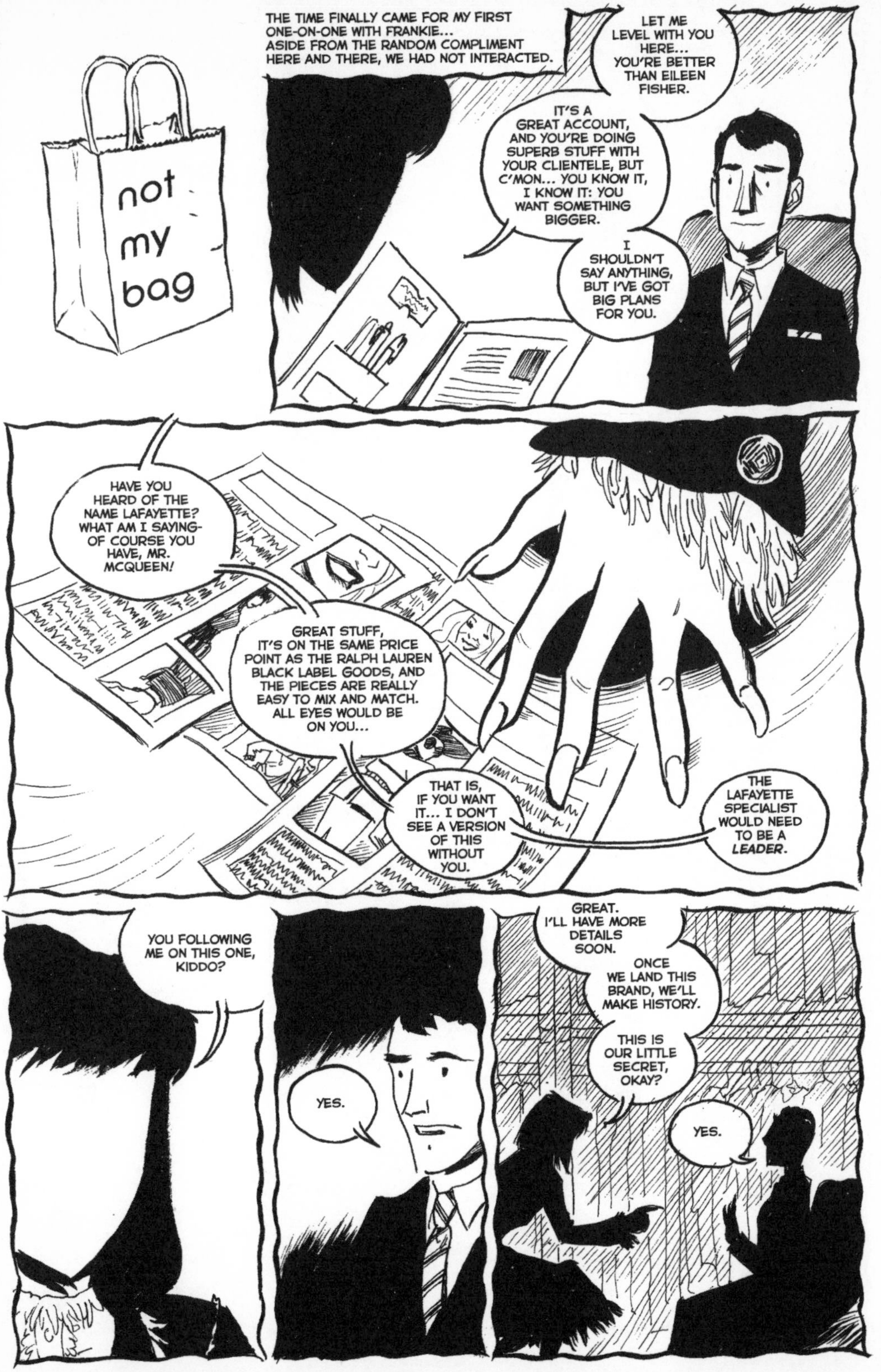
not my bag
THE TIME FINALLY CAME FOR MY FIRST ONE-ON-ONE WITH FRANKIE... ASIDE FROM THE RANDOM COMPLIMENT HERE AND THERE, WE HAD NOT INTERACTED.
LET ME LEVEL WITH YOU HERE... YOU'RE BETTER THAN EILEEN FISHER.
IT'S A GREAT ACCOUNT, AND YOU'RE DOING SUPERB STUFF WITH YOUR CLIENTELE, BUT C'MON... YOU KNOW IT, I KNOW IT: YOU WANT SOMETHING BIGGER.
I SHOULDN'T SAY ANYTHING, BUT I'VE GOT BIG PLANS FOR YOU.
HAVE YOU HEARD OF THE NAME LAFAYETTE? WHAT AM I SAYING- OF COURSE YOU HAVE, MR. MCQUEEN!
GREAT STUFF, IT'S ON THE SAME PRICE POINT AS THE RALPH LAUREN BLACK LABEL GOODS, AND THE PIECES ARE REALLY EASY TO MIX AND MATCH. ALL EYES WOULD BE ON YOU...
THAT IS, IF YOU WANT IT... I DON'T SEE A VERSION OF THIS WITHOUT YOU.
THE LAFAYETTE SPECIALIST WOULD NEED TO BE A *LEADER*.
YOU FOLLOWING ME ON THIS ONE, KIDDO?
YES.
GREAT. I'LL HAVE MORE DETAILS SOON.
ONCE WE LAND THIS BRAND, WE'LL MAKE HISTORY.
THIS IS OUR LITTLE SECRET, OKAY?
YES.

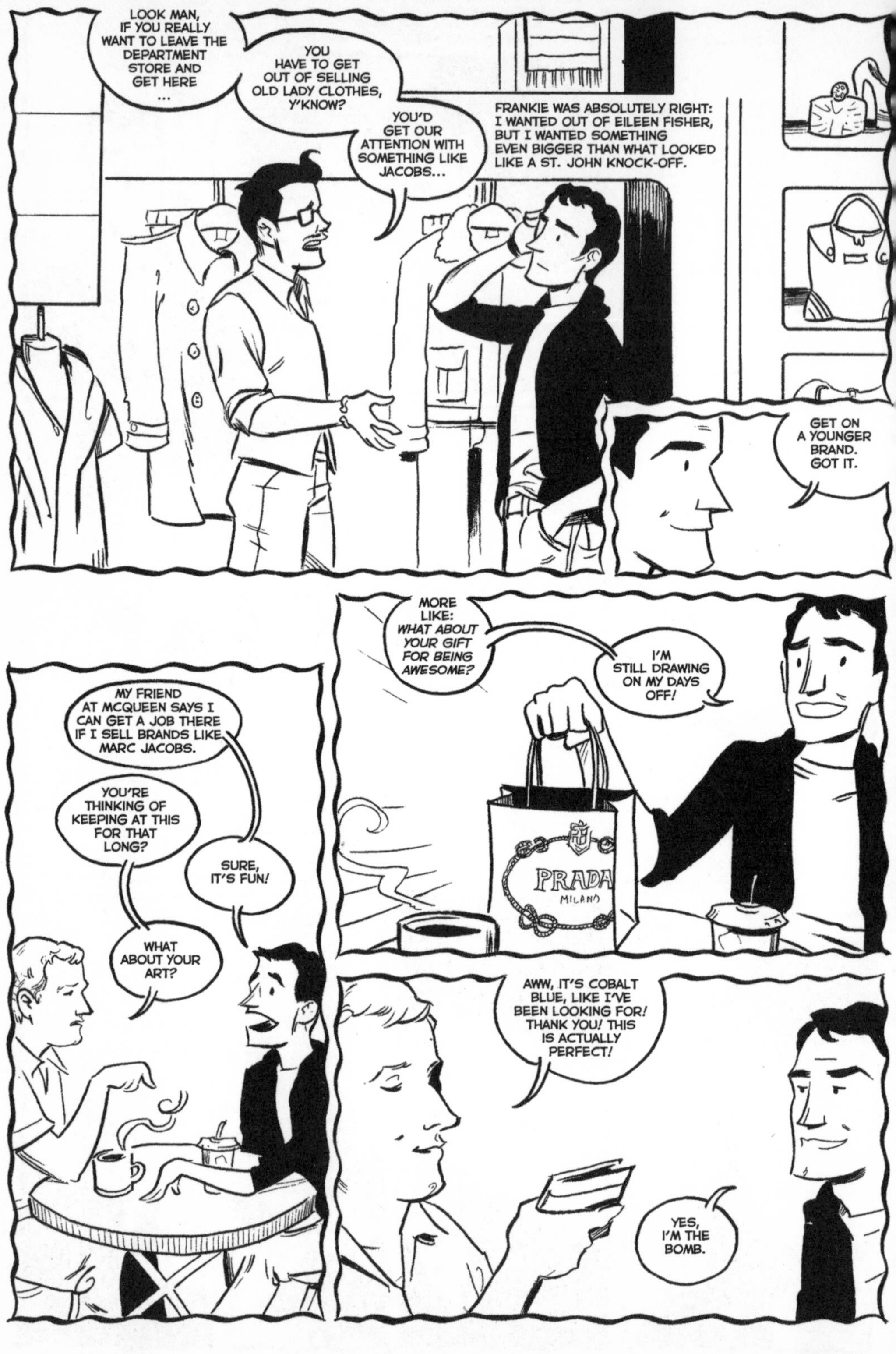
LOOK MAN, IF YOU REALLY WANT TO LEAVE THE DEPARTMENT STORE AND GET HERE ...
YOU HAVE TO GET OUT OF SELLING OLD LADY CLOTHES, Y'KNOW?
YOU'D GET OUR ATTENTION WITH SOMETHING LIKE JACOBS...
FRANKIE WAS ABSOLUTELY RIGHT: I WANTED OUT OF EILEEN FISHER, BUT I WANTED SOMETHING EVEN BIGGER THAN WHAT LOOKED LIKE A ST. JOHN KNOCK-OFF.
GET ON A YOUNGER BRAND. GOT IT.
MY FRIEND AT MCQUEEN SAYS I CAN GET A JOB THERE IF I SELL BRANDS LIKE MARC JACOBS.
YOU'RE THINKING OF KEEPING AT THIS FOR THAT LONG?
SURE, IT'S FUN!
WHAT ABOUT YOUR ART?
MORE LIKE: *WHAT ABOUT YOUR GIFT FOR BEING AWESOME?*
I'M STILL DRAWING ON MY DAYS OFF!
PRADA
MILANO
AWW, IT'S COBALT BLUE, LIKE I'VE BEEN LOOKING FOR! THANK YOU! THIS IS ACTUALLY PERFECT!
YES, I'M THE BOMB.

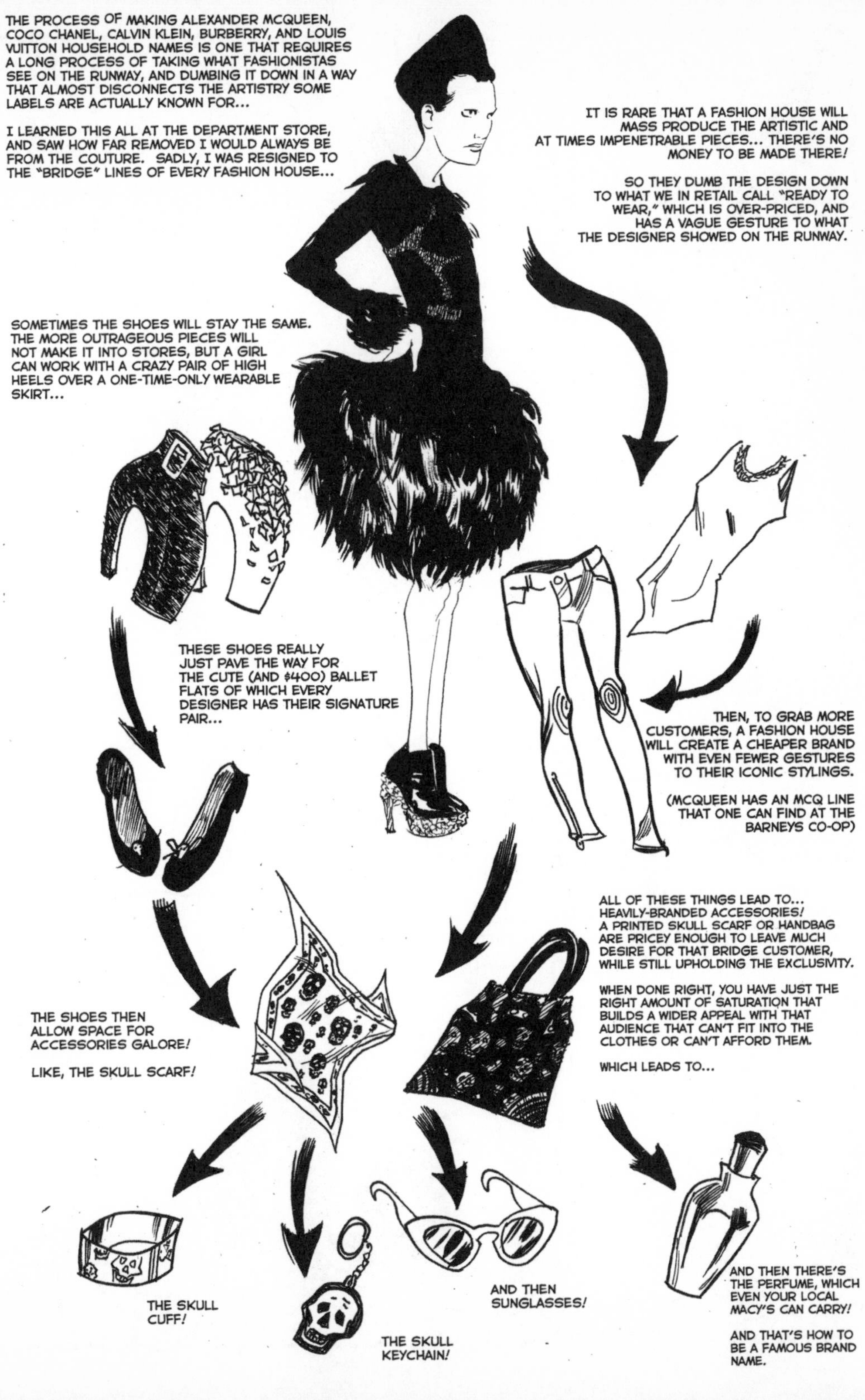
THE PROCESS OF MAKING ALEXANDER MCQUEEN, COCO CHANEL, CALVIN KLEIN, BURBERRY, AND LOUIS VUITTON HOUSEHOLD NAMES IS ONE THAT REQUIRES A LONG PROCESS OF TAKING WHAT FASHIONISTAS SEE ON THE RUNWAY, AND DUMBING IT DOWN IN A WAY THAT ALMOST DISCONNECTS THE ARTISTRY SOME LABELS ARE ACTUALLY KNOWN FOR...
I LEARNED THIS ALL AT THE DEPARTMENT STORE, AND SAW HOW FAR REMOVED I WOULD ALWAYS BE FROM THE COUTURE. SADLY, I WAS RESIGNED TO THE "BRIDGE" LINES OF EVERY FASHION HOUSE...
IT IS RARE THAT A FASHION HOUSE WILL MASS PRODUCE THE ARTISTIC AND AT TIMES IMPENETRABLE PIECES... THERE'S NO MONEY TO BE MADE THERE!
SO THEY DUMB THE DESIGN DOWN TO WHAT WE IN RETAIL CALL "READY TO WEAR," WHICH IS OVER-PRICED, AND HAS A VAGUE GESTURE TO WHAT THE DESIGNER SHOWED ON THE RUNWAY.
SOMETIMES THE SHOES WILL STAY THE SAME. THE MORE OUTRAGEOUS PIECES WILL NOT MAKE IT INTO STORES, BUT A GIRL CAN WORK WITH A CRAZY PAIR OF HIGH HEELS OVER A ONE-TIME-ONLY WEARABLE SKIRT...
THESE SHOES REALLY JUST PAVE THE WAY FOR THE CUTE (AND $400) BALLET FLATS OF WHICH EVERY DESIGNER HAS THEIR SIGNATURE PAIR...
THEN, TO GRAB MORE CUSTOMERS, A FASHION HOUSE WILL CREATE A CHEAPER BRAND WITH EVEN FEWER GESTURES TO THEIR ICONIC STYLINGS.
(MCQUEEN HAS AN MCQ LINE THAT ONE CAN FIND AT THE BARNEYS CO-OP)
ALL OF THESE THINGS LEAD TO... HEAVILY-BRANDED ACCESSORIES! A PRINTED SKULL SCARF OR HANDBAG ARE PRICEY ENOUGH TO LEAVE MUCH DESIRE FOR THAT BRIDGE CUSTOMER, WHILE STILL UPHOLDING THE EXCLUSIVITY.
WHEN DONE RIGHT, YOU HAVE JUST THE RIGHT AMOUNT OF SATURATION THAT BUILDS A WIDER APPEAL WITH THAT AUDIENCE THAT CAN'T FIT INTO THE CLOTHES OR CAN'T AFFORD THEM.
WHICH LEADS TO...
THE SHOES THEN ALLOW SPACE FOR ACCESSORIES GALORE!
LIKE, THE SKULL SCARF!
THE SKULL CUFF!
THE SKULL KEYCHAIN!
AND THEN SUNGLASSES!
AND THEN THERE'S THE PERFUME, WHICH EVEN YOUR LOCAL MACY'S CAN CARRY!
AND THAT'S HOW TO BE A FAMOUS BRAND NAME.

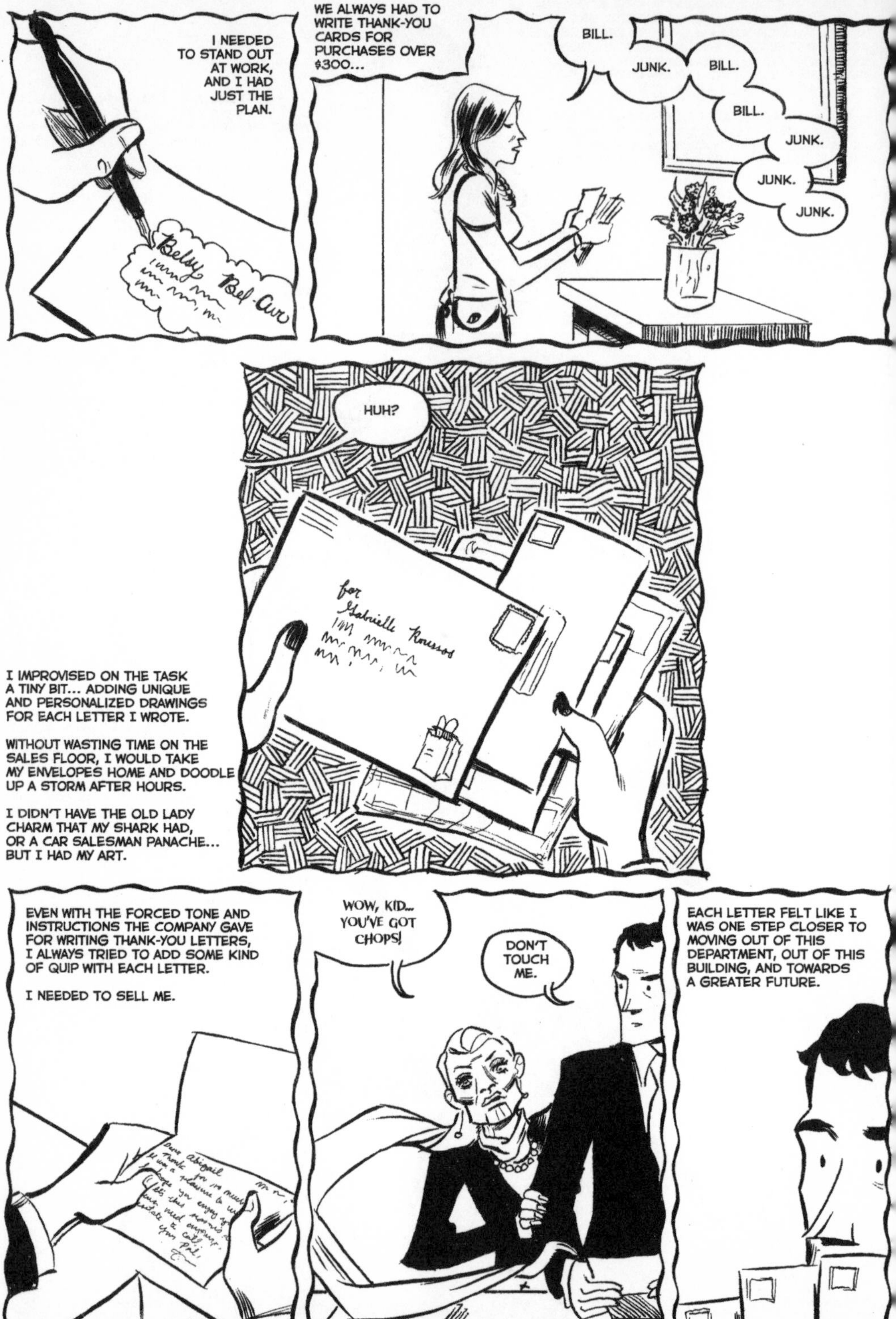

I NEEDED TO STAND OUT AT WORK, AND I HAD JUST THE PLAN.
WE ALWAYS HAD TO WRITE THANK-YOU CARDS FOR PURCHASES OVER $300...
BILL.
JUNK.
BILL.
BILL.
JUNK.
JUNK.
JUNK.
HUH?
I IMPROVISED ON THE TASK A TINY BIT... ADDING UNIQUE AND PERSONALIZED DRAWINGS FOR EACH LETTER I WROTE.
WITHOUT WASTING TIME ON THE SALES FLOOR, I WOULD TAKE MY ENVELOPES HOME AND DOODLE UP A STORM AFTER HOURS.
I DIDN'T HAVE THE OLD LADY CHARM THAT MY SHARK HAD, OR A CAR SALESMAN PANACHE... BUT I HAD MY ART.
EVEN WITH THE FORCED TONE AND INSTRUCTIONS THE COMPANY GAVE FOR WRITING THANK-YOU LETTERS, I ALWAYS TRIED TO ADD SOME KIND OF QUIP WITH EACH LETTER.
I NEEDED TO SELL ME.
WOW, KID... YOU'VE GOT CHOPS!
DON'T TOUCH ME.
EACH LETTER FELT LIKE I WAS ONE STEP CLOSER TO MOVING OUT OF THIS DEPARTMENT, OUT OF THIS BUILDING, AND TOWARDS A GREATER FUTURE.

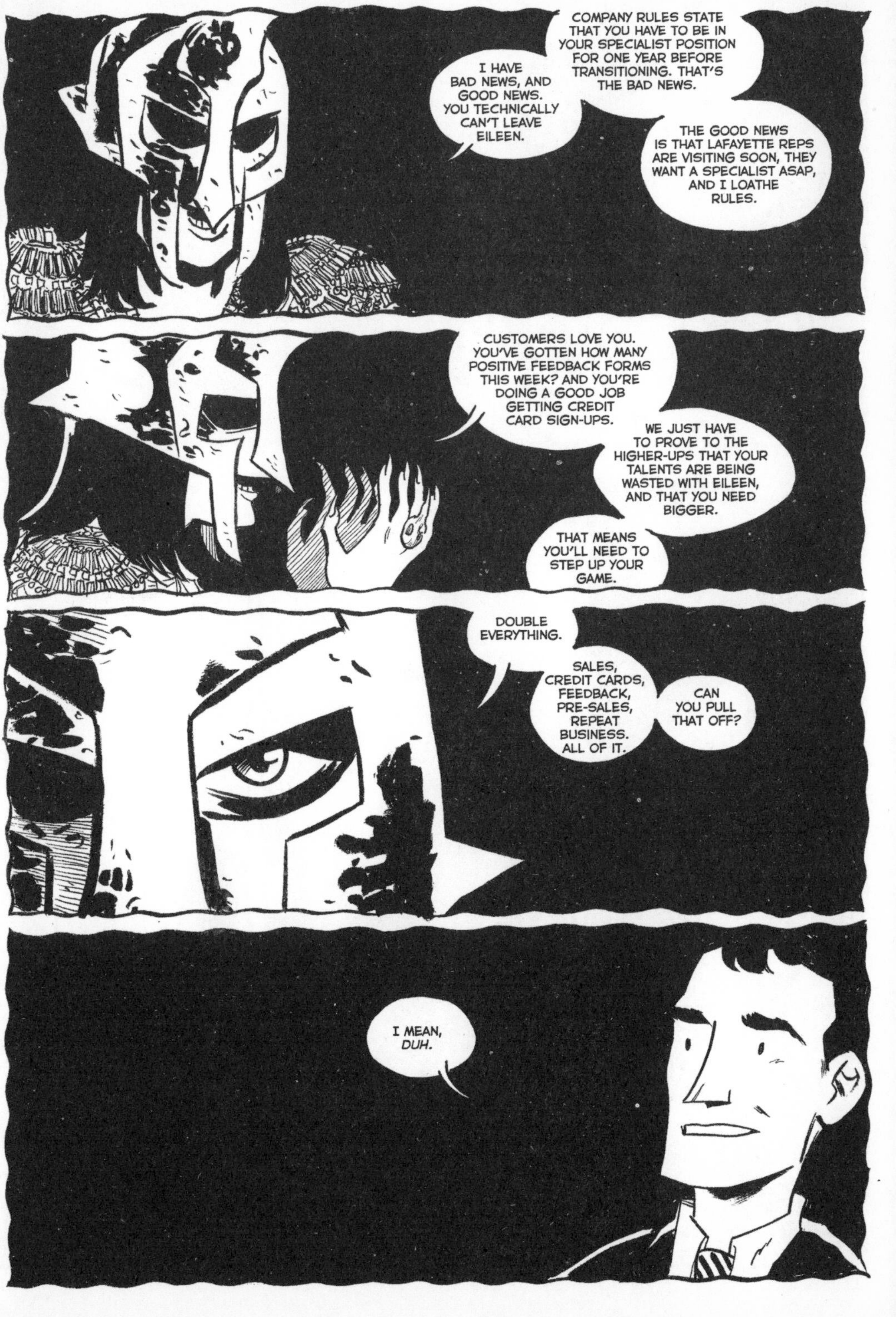
I HAVE BAD NEWS, AND GOOD NEWS. YOU TECHNICALLY CAN'T LEAVE EILEEN.
COMPANY RULES STATE THAT YOU HAVE TO BE IN YOUR SPECIALIST POSITION FOR ONE YEAR BEFORE TRANSITIONING. THAT'S THE BAD NEWS.
THE GOOD NEWS IS THAT LAFAYETTE REPS ARE VISITING SOON, THEY WANT A SPECIALIST ASAP, AND I LOATHE RULES.
CUSTOMERS LOVE YOU. YOU'VE GOTTEN HOW MANY POSITIVE FEEDBACK FORMS THIS WEEK? AND YOU'RE DOING A GOOD JOB GETTING CREDIT CARD SIGN-UPS.
WE JUST HAVE TO PROVE TO THE HIGHER-UPS THAT YOUR TALENTS ARE BEING WASTED WITH EILEEN, AND THAT YOU NEED BIGGER.
THAT MEANS YOU'LL NEED TO STEP UP YOUR GAME.
DOUBLE EVERYTHING.
SALES, CREDIT CARDS, FEEDBACK, PRE-SALES, REPEAT BUSINESS. ALL OF IT.
CAN YOU PULL THAT OFF?
I MEAN, *DUH.*

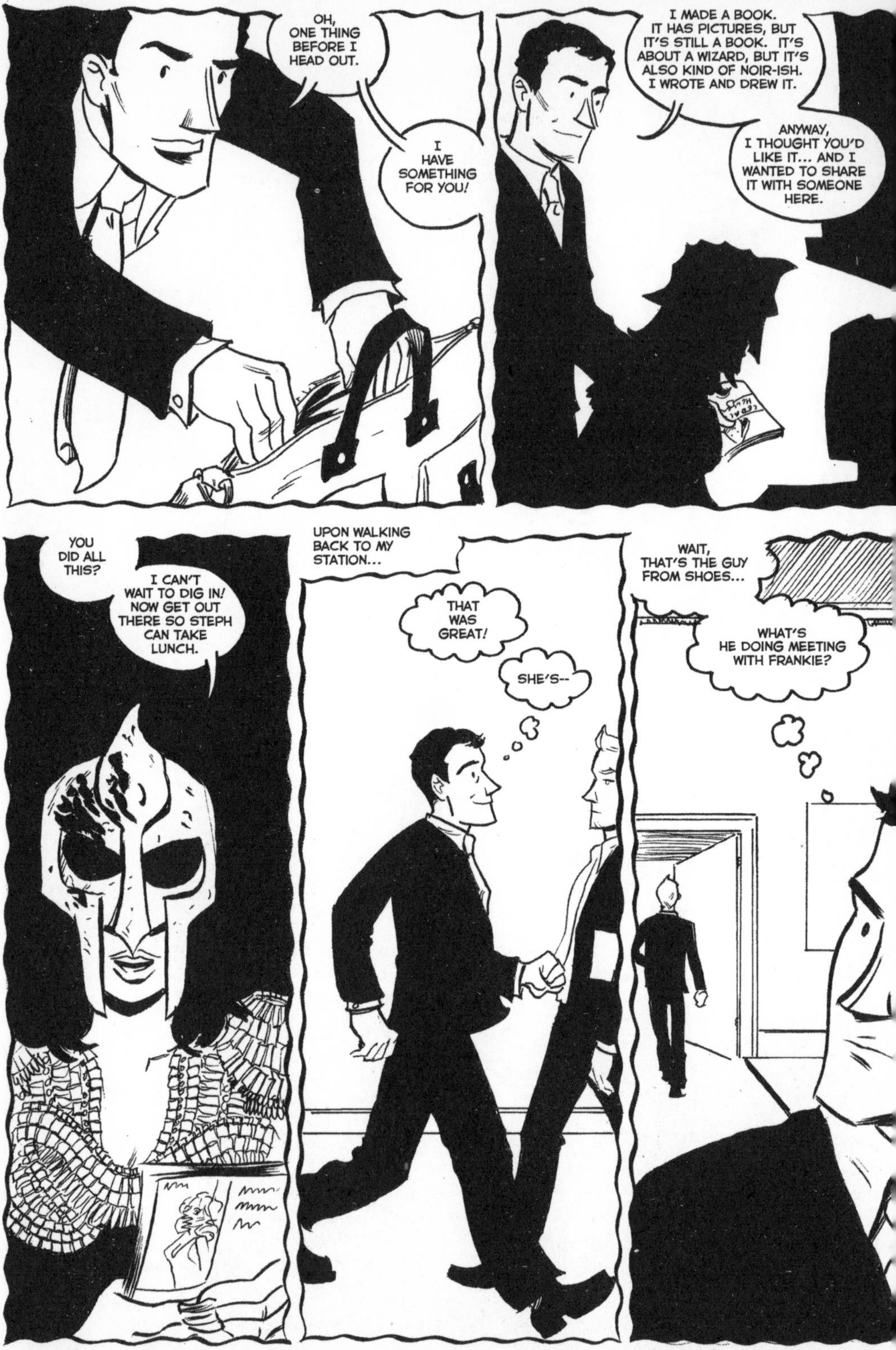
OH, ONE THING BEFORE I HEAD OUT.
I HAVE SOMETHING FOR YOU!
I MADE A BOOK. IT HAS PICTURES, BUT IT'S STILL A BOOK. IT'S ABOUT A WIZARD, BUT IT'S ALSO KIND OF NOIR-ISH. I WROTE AND DREW IT.
ANYWAY, I THOUGHT YOU'D LIKE IT... AND I WANTED TO SHARE IT WITH SOMEONE HERE.
YOU DID ALL THIS?
I CAN'T WAIT TO DIG IN! NOW GET OUT THERE SO STEPH CAN TAKE LUNCH.
UPON WALKING BACK TO MY STATION...
THAT WAS GREAT!
SHE'S--
WAIT, THAT'S THE GUY FROM SHOES...
WHAT'S HE DOING MEETING WITH FRANKIE?

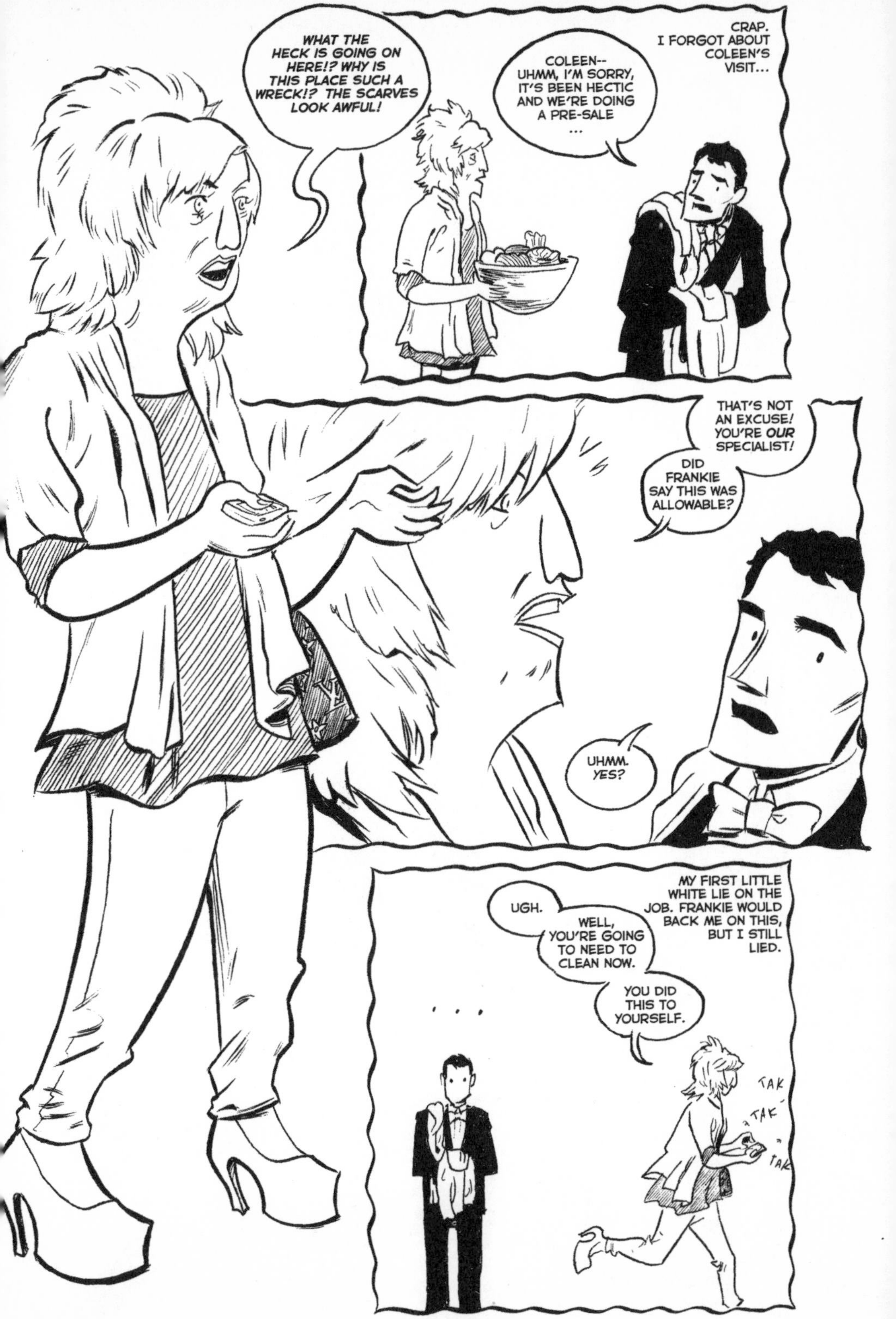
WHAT THE HECK IS GOING ON HERE!? WHY IS THIS PLACE SUCH A WRECK!? THE SCARVES LOOK AWFUL!
CRAP. I FORGOT ABOUT COLEEN'S VISIT...
COLEEN-- UHMM, I'M SORRY, IT'S BEEN HECTIC AND WE'RE DOING A PRE-SALE ...
THAT'S NOT AN EXCUSE! YOU'RE OUR SPECIALIST!
DID FRANKIE SAY THIS WAS ALLOWABLE?
UHMM. YES?
MY FIRST LITTLE WHITE LIE ON THE JOB. FRANKIE WOULD BACK ME ON THIS, BUT I STILL LIED.
UGH.
WELL, YOU'RE GOING TO NEED TO CLEAN NOW.
YOU DID THIS TO YOURSELF.
. . .
TAK
TAK
TAK

MY WARDROBE- LIKE MY LIFE- HAD BECOME COMPARTMENTALIZED INTO THREE SECTIONS: WORK, PLAY, AND ART. AT POINTS, I FELT LIKE A PAPER DOLL THAT HAD A SIMPLE ASSORTMENT OF CLOTHES TO PICK, ALL YOU HAD TO DO WAS FOLD THE CORNERS AROUND MY SHOULDERS, AND I WOULD BE READY FOR THE WORLD.

1) WORK: BLACK SUIT, CLEAN BUTTON-DOWN SHIRT, AND SOME SNAZZY TIE.

2) PLAY: RAGS! RAGS! RAGS! STYLISH-YET-TATTERED CLOTHES I CAN RUN AROUND TOWN IN FREE!

3) ART: FOR EVENTS, EVENINGS OUT, OR WHEN I FELT LIKE PUSHING THE BOUNDARIES OF MY PERSONAL TASTE, I WENT FOR STYLE AND EXPERIMENTATION.

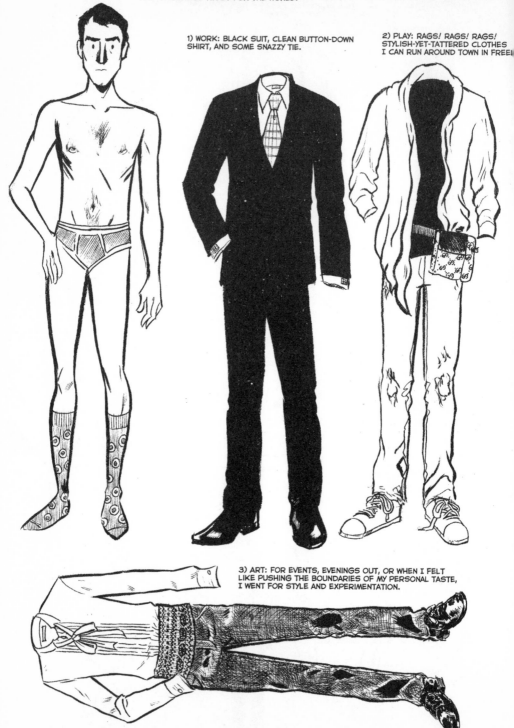

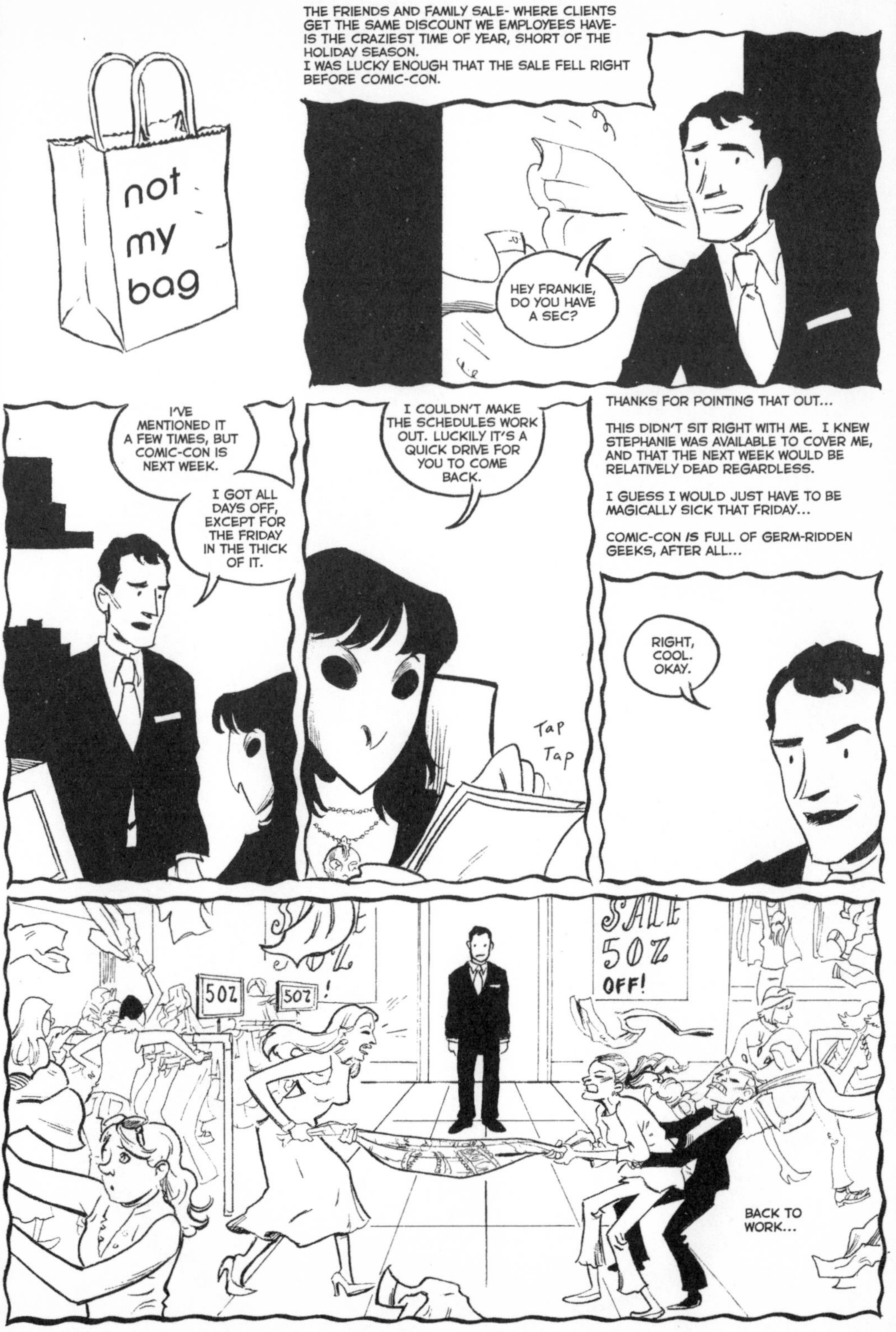

not my bag
THE FRIENDS AND FAMILY SALE- WHERE CLIENTS GET THE SAME DISCOUNT WE EMPLOYEES HAVE- IS THE CRAZIEST TIME OF YEAR, SHORT OF THE HOLIDAY SEASON.
I WAS LUCKY ENOUGH THAT THE SALE FELL RIGHT BEFORE COMIC-CON.
HEY FRANKIE, DO YOU HAVE A SEC?
I'VE MENTIONED IT A FEW TIMES, BUT COMIC-CON IS NEXT WEEK.
I GOT ALL DAYS OFF, EXCEPT FOR THE FRIDAY IN THE THICK OF IT.
I COULDN'T MAKE THE SCHEDULES WORK OUT. LUCKILY IT'S A QUICK DRIVE FOR YOU TO COME BACK.
Tap Tap
THANKS FOR POINTING THAT OUT...
THIS DIDN'T SIT RIGHT WITH ME. I KNEW STEPHANIE WAS AVAILABLE TO COVER ME, AND THAT THE NEXT WEEK WOULD BE RELATIVELY DEAD REGARDLESS.
I GUESS I WOULD JUST HAVE TO BE MAGICALLY SICK THAT FRIDAY...
COMIC-CON *IS* FULL OF GERM-RIDDEN GEEKS, AFTER ALL...
RIGHT, COOL. OKAY.
50%
50%
SALE 50% OFF!
BACK TO WORK...

IT HAPPENED: I WAS FRANKIE'S TOY.
I HAD BECOME THE PERSON I HATED MOST, ALL FOR THE NOTION OF A PROMOTION. I COULD LIE TO MYSELF AND SAY I DID EVERYTHING BECAUSE I WAS TRYING TO FIND A BETTER JOB OUTSIDE OF THE DEPARTMENT STORE, BUT YOU HAD TO WONDER: WHY WAS I TRYING SO HARD IN A PROFESSION I TECHNICALLY WASN'T GOING TO STICK AROUND FOR?

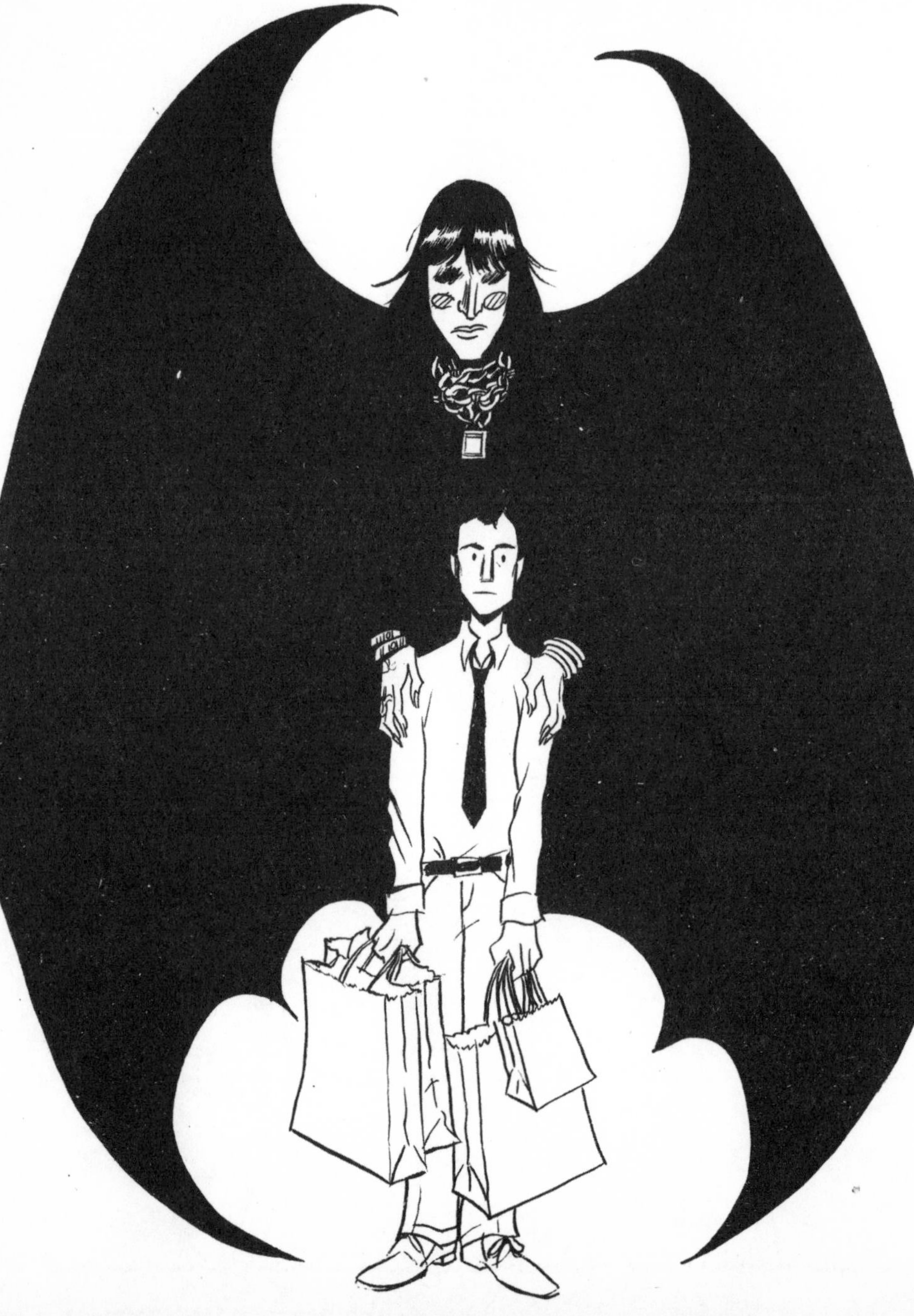

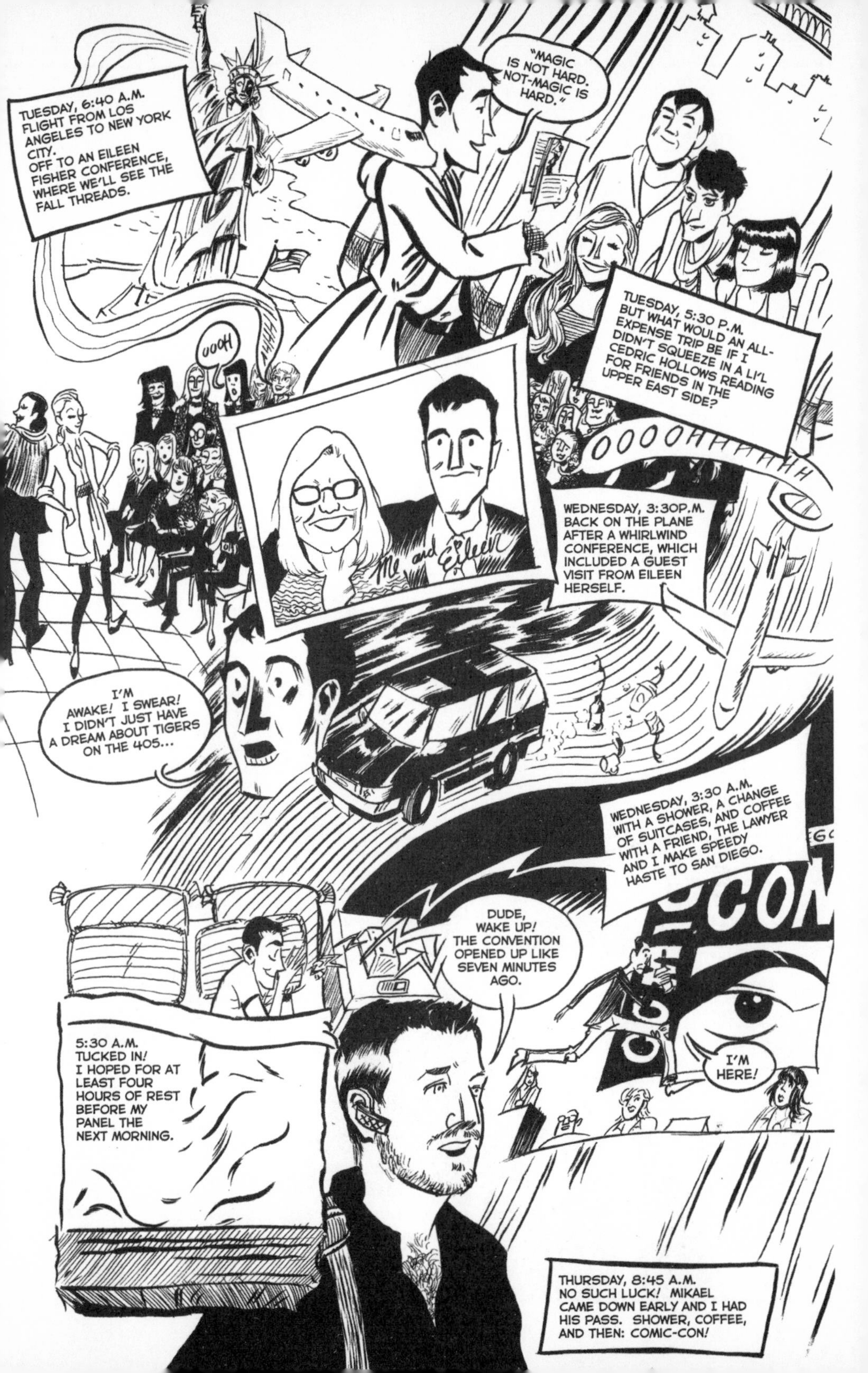
TUESDAY, 6:40 A.M. FLIGHT FROM LOS ANGELES TO NEW YORK CITY. OFF TO AN EILEEN FISHER CONFERENCE, WHERE WE'LL SEE THE FALL THREADS.
"MAGIC IS NOT HARD. NOT-MAGIC IS HARD."
OOOH
AHHH
TUESDAY, 5:30 P.M. BUT WHAT WOULD AN ALL-EXPENSE TRIP BE IF I DIDN'T SQUEEZE IN A LI'L CEDRIC HOLLOWS READING FOR FRIENDS IN THE UPPER EAST SIDE?
Me and Eileen
OOOOHHHHHHH
WEDNESDAY, 3:30P.M. BACK ON THE PLANE AFTER A WHIRLWIND CONFERENCE, WHICH INCLUDED A GUEST VISIT FROM EILEEN HERSELF.
I'M AWAKE! I SWEAR! I DIDN'T JUST HAVE A DREAM ABOUT TIGERS ON THE 405...
WEDNESDAY, 3:30 A.M. WITH A SHOWER, A CHANGE OF SUITCASES, AND COFFEE WITH A FRIEND, THE LAWYER AND I MAKE SPEEDY HASTE TO SAN DIEGO.
CON
DUDE, WAKE UP! THE CONVENTION OPENED UP LIKE SEVEN MINUTES AGO.
5:30 A.M. TUCKED IN! I HOPED FOR AT LEAST FOUR HOURS OF REST BEFORE MY PANEL THE NEXT MORNING.
I'M HERE!
THURSDAY, 8:45 A.M. NO SUCH LUCK! MIKAEL CAME DOWN EARLY AND I HAD HIS PASS. SHOWER, COFFEE, AND THEN: COMIC-CON!

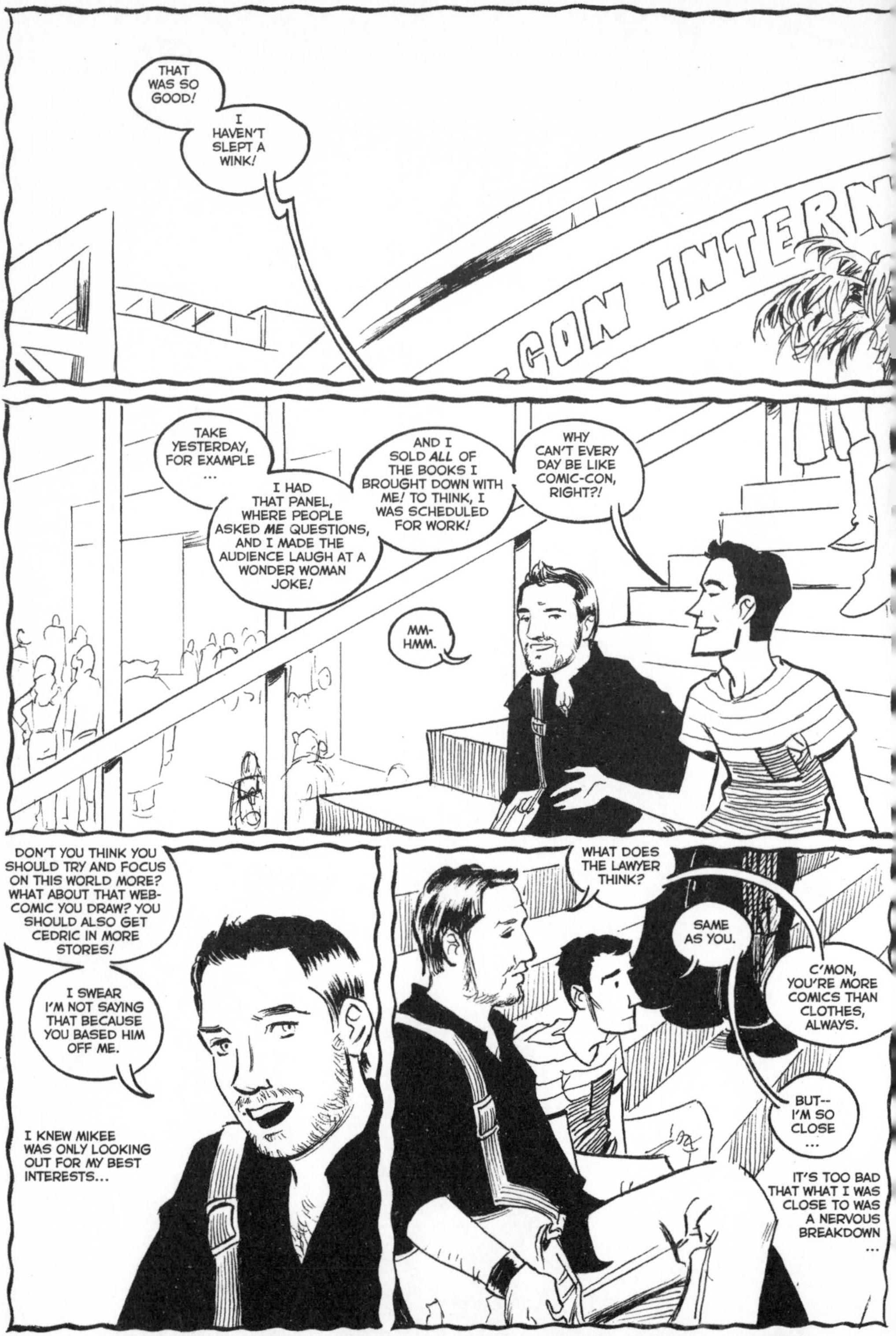

THAT WAS SO GOOD!
I HAVEN'T SLEPT A WINK!
CON INTERN
TAKE YESTERDAY, FOR EXAMPLE ...
I HAD THAT PANEL, WHERE PEOPLE ASKED *ME* QUESTIONS, AND I MADE THE AUDIENCE LAUGH AT A WONDER WOMAN JOKE!
AND I SOLD *ALL* OF THE BOOKS I BROUGHT DOWN WITH ME! TO THINK, I WAS SCHEDULED FOR WORK!
WHY CAN'T EVERY DAY BE LIKE COMIC-CON, RIGHT?!
MM-HMM.
DON'T YOU THINK YOU SHOULD TRY AND FOCUS ON THIS WORLD MORE? WHAT ABOUT THAT WEB-COMIC YOU DRAW? YOU SHOULD ALSO GET CEDRIC IN MORE STORES!
I SWEAR I'M NOT SAYING THAT BECAUSE YOU BASED HIM OFF ME.
I KNEW MIKEE WAS ONLY LOOKING OUT FOR MY BEST INTERESTS...
WHAT DOES THE LAWYER THINK?
SAME AS YOU.
C'MON, YOU'RE MORE COMICS THAN CLOTHES, ALWAYS.
BUT-- I'M SO CLOSE ...
IT'S TOO BAD THAT WHAT I WAS CLOSE TO WAS A NERVOUS BREAKDOWN ...

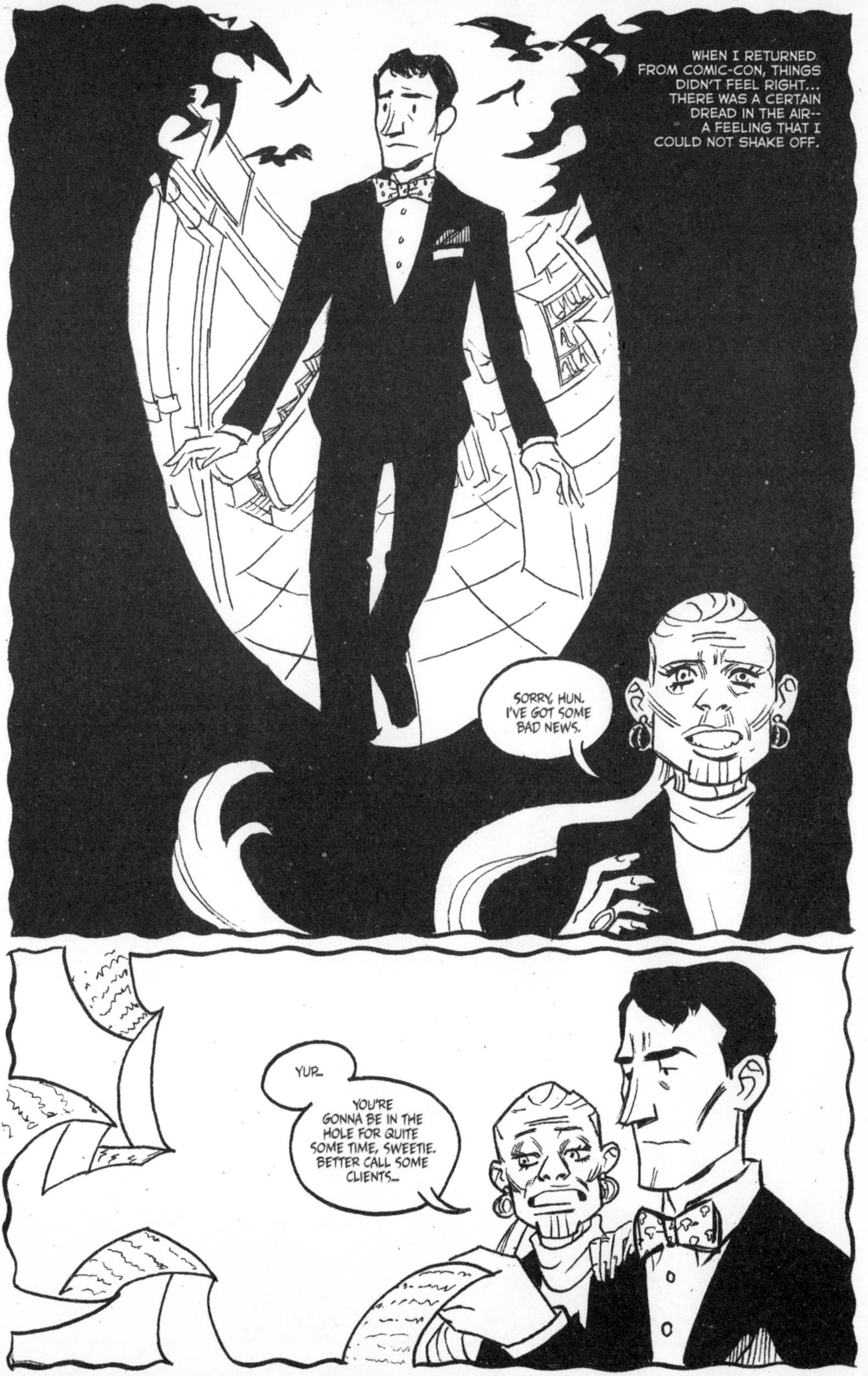
WHEN I RETURNED FROM COMIC-CON, THINGS DIDN'T FEEL RIGHT... THERE WAS A CERTAIN DREAD IN THE AIR-- A FEELING THAT I COULD NOT SHAKE OFF.
SORRY, HUN. I'VE GOT SOME BAD NEWS.
YUP...
YOU'RE GONNA BE IN THE HOLE FOR QUITE SOME TIME, SWEETIE. BETTER CALL SOME CLIENTS...

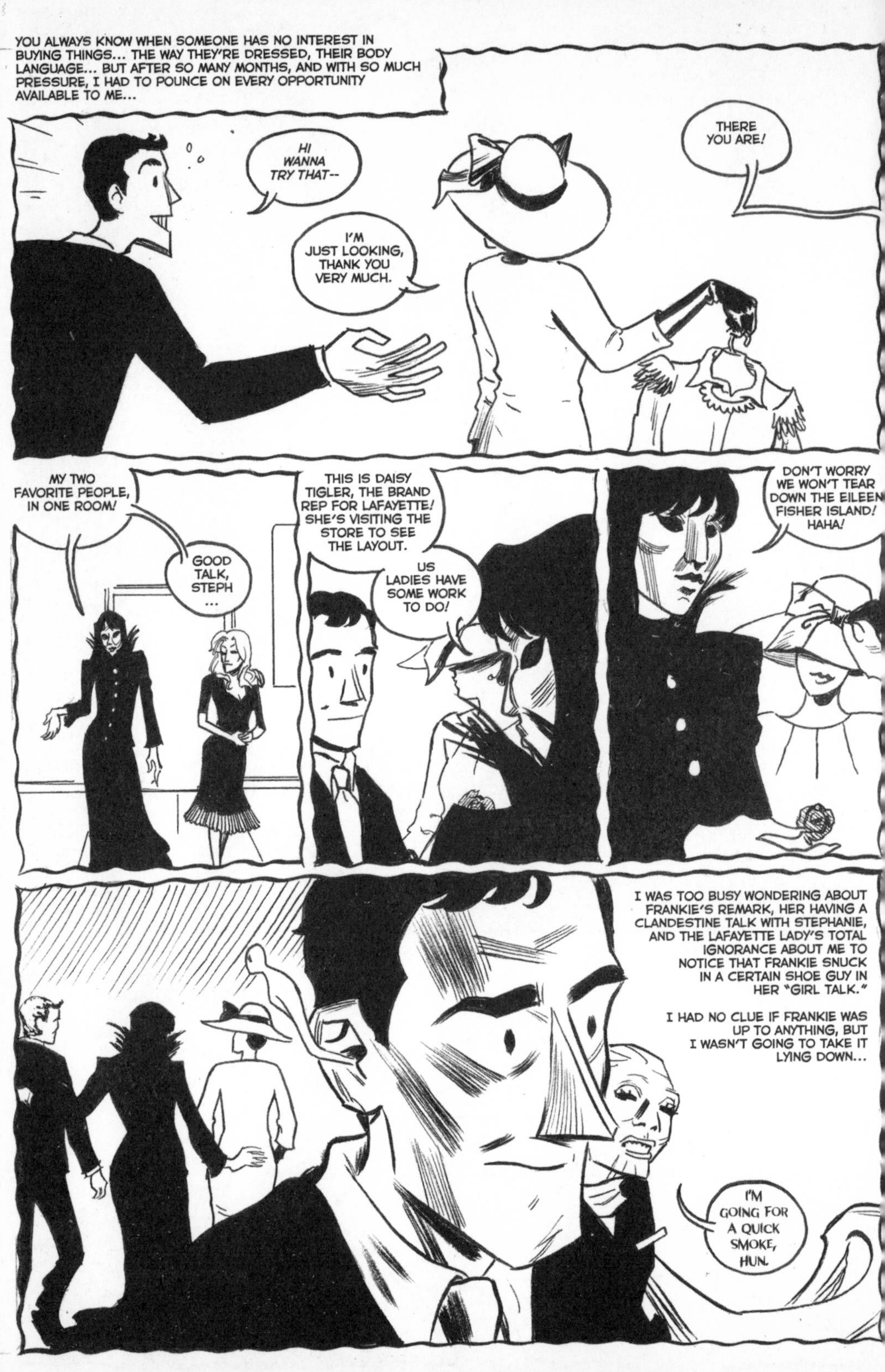
YOU ALWAYS KNOW WHEN SOMEONE HAS NO INTEREST IN BUYING THINGS... THE WAY THEY'RE DRESSED, THEIR BODY LANGUAGE... BUT AFTER SO MANY MONTHS, AND WITH SO MUCH PRESSURE, I HAD TO POUNCE ON EVERY OPPORTUNITY AVAILABLE TO ME...
HI WANNA TRY THAT--
I'M JUST LOOKING, THANK YOU VERY MUCH.
THERE YOU ARE!
MY TWO FAVORITE PEOPLE, IN ONE ROOM!
GOOD TALK, STEPH ...
THIS IS DAISY TIGLER, THE BRAND REP FOR LAFAYETTE! SHE'S VISITING THE STORE TO SEE THE LAYOUT.
US LADIES HAVE SOME WORK TO DO!
DON'T WORRY WE WON'T TEAR DOWN THE EILEEN FISHER ISLAND! HAHA!
I WAS TOO BUSY WONDERING ABOUT FRANKIE'S REMARK, HER HAVING A CLANDESTINE TALK WITH STEPHANIE, AND THE LAFAYETTE LADY'S TOTAL IGNORANCE ABOUT ME TO NOTICE THAT FRANKIE SNUCK IN A CERTAIN SHOE GUY IN HER "GIRL TALK."
I HAD NO CLUE IF FRANKIE WAS UP TO ANYTHING, BUT I WASN'T GOING TO TAKE IT LYING DOWN...
I'M GOING FOR A QUICK SMOKE, HUN.

chapter
three

"The bastard form of mass culture is humiliated repetition... always new books, new programs, new films, news items, but always the same meaning."

--Roland Barthes

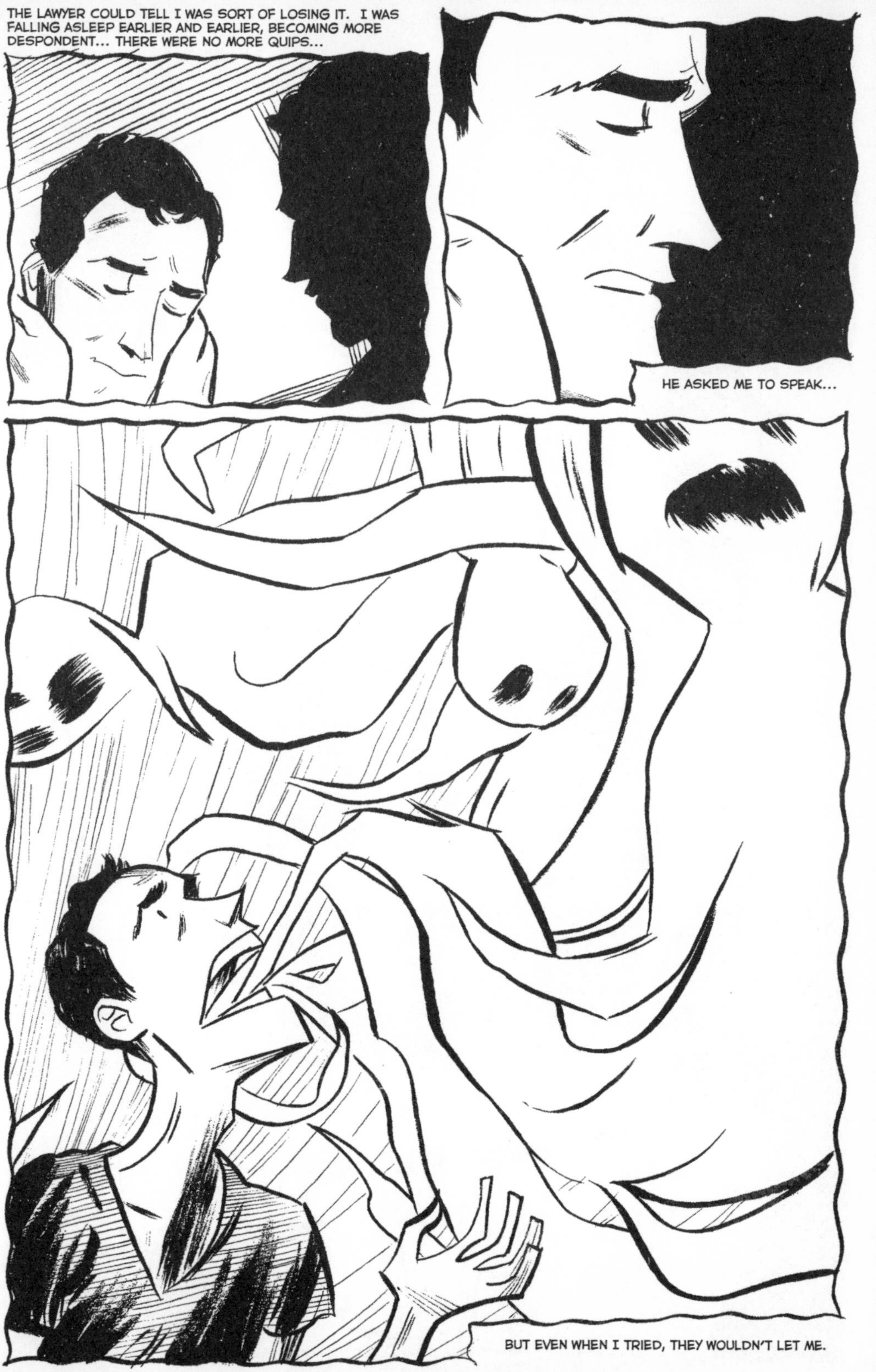
THE LAWYER COULD TELL I WAS SORT OF LOSING IT. I WAS FALLING ASLEEP EARLIER AND EARLIER, BECOMING MORE DESPONDENT... THERE WERE NO MORE QUIPS...
HE ASKED ME TO SPEAK...
BUT EVEN WHEN I TRIED, THEY WOULDN'T LET ME.

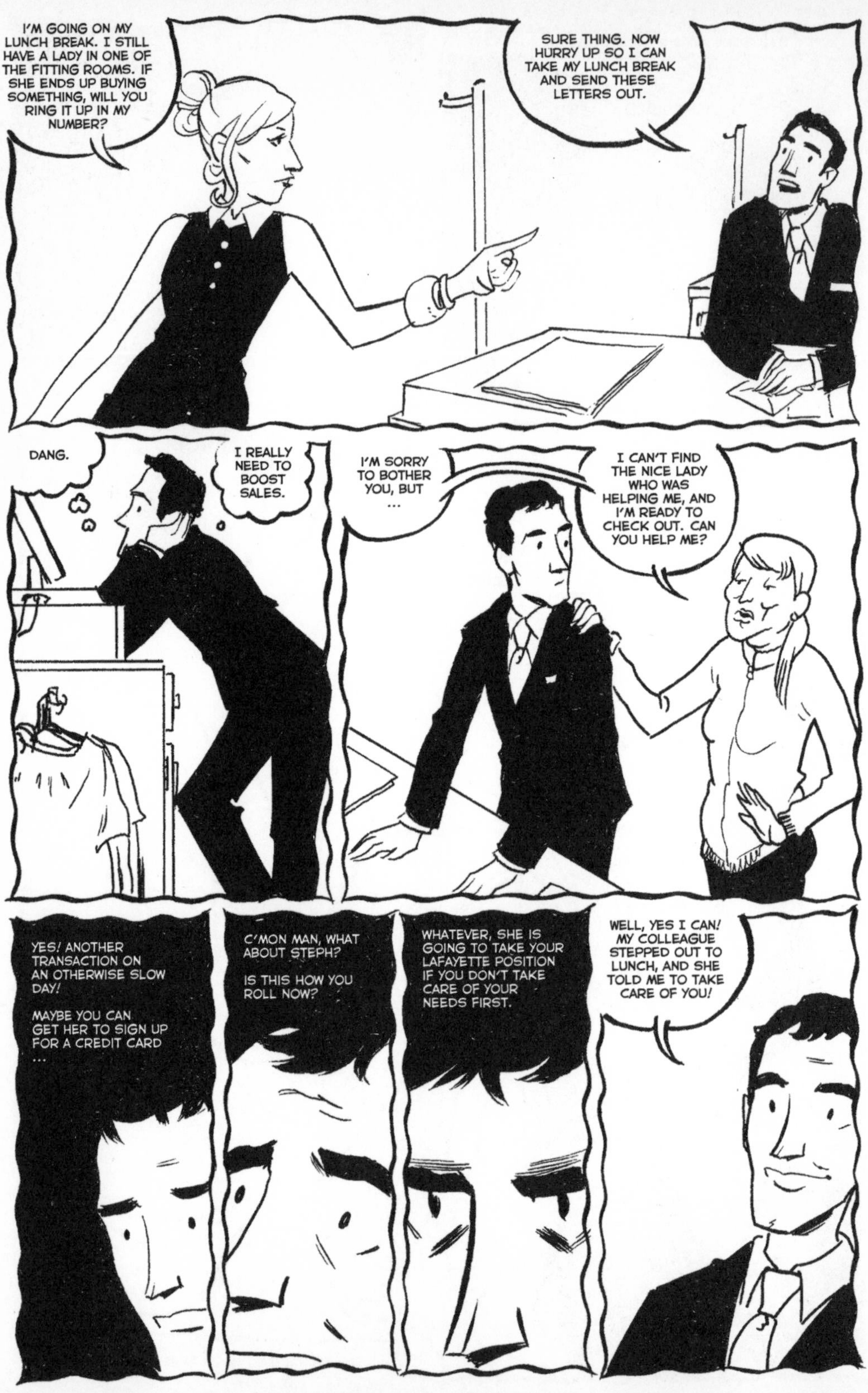
I'M GOING ON MY LUNCH BREAK. I STILL HAVE A LADY IN ONE OF THE FITTING ROOMS. IF SHE ENDS UP BUYING SOMETHING, WILL YOU RING IT UP IN MY NUMBER?
SURE THING. NOW HURRY UP SO I CAN TAKE MY LUNCH BREAK AND SEND THESE LETTERS OUT.
DANG.
I REALLY NEED TO BOOST SALES.
I'M SORRY TO BOTHER YOU, BUT ...
I CAN'T FIND THE NICE LADY WHO WAS HELPING ME, AND I'M READY TO CHECK OUT. CAN YOU HELP ME?
YES! ANOTHER TRANSACTION ON AN OTHERWISE SLOW DAY!
MAYBE YOU CAN GET HER TO SIGN UP FOR A CREDIT CARD ...
C'MON MAN, WHAT ABOUT STEPH?
IS THIS HOW YOU ROLL NOW?
WHATEVER, SHE IS GOING TO TAKE YOUR LAFAYETTE POSITION IF YOU DON'T TAKE CARE OF YOUR NEEDS FIRST.
WELL, YES I CAN! MY COLLEAGUE STEPPED OUT TO LUNCH, AND SHE TOLD ME TO TAKE CARE OF YOU!

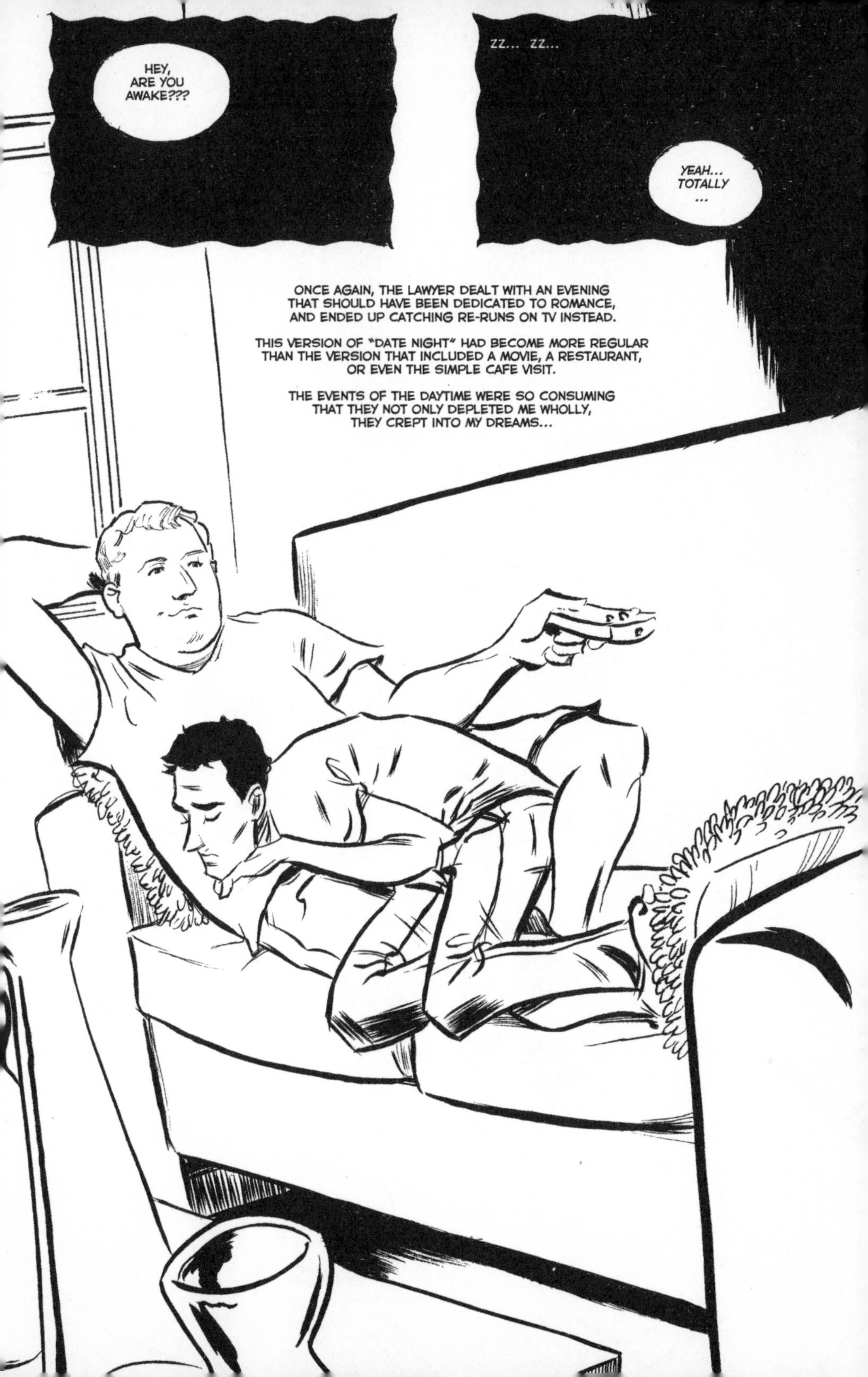
HEY, ARE YOU AWAKE???
ZZ... ZZ...
YEAH... TOTALLY ...
ONCE AGAIN, THE LAWYER DEALT WITH AN EVENING THAT SHOULD HAVE BEEN DEDICATED TO ROMANCE, AND ENDED UP CATCHING RE-RUNS ON TV INSTEAD.
THIS VERSION OF "DATE NIGHT" HAD BECOME MORE REGULAR THAN THE VERSION THAT INCLUDED A MOVIE, A RESTAURANT, OR EVEN THE SIMPLE CAFE VISIT.
THE EVENTS OF THE DAYTIME WERE SO CONSUMING THAT THEY NOT ONLY DEPLETED ME WHOLLY, THEY CREPT INTO MY DREAMS...

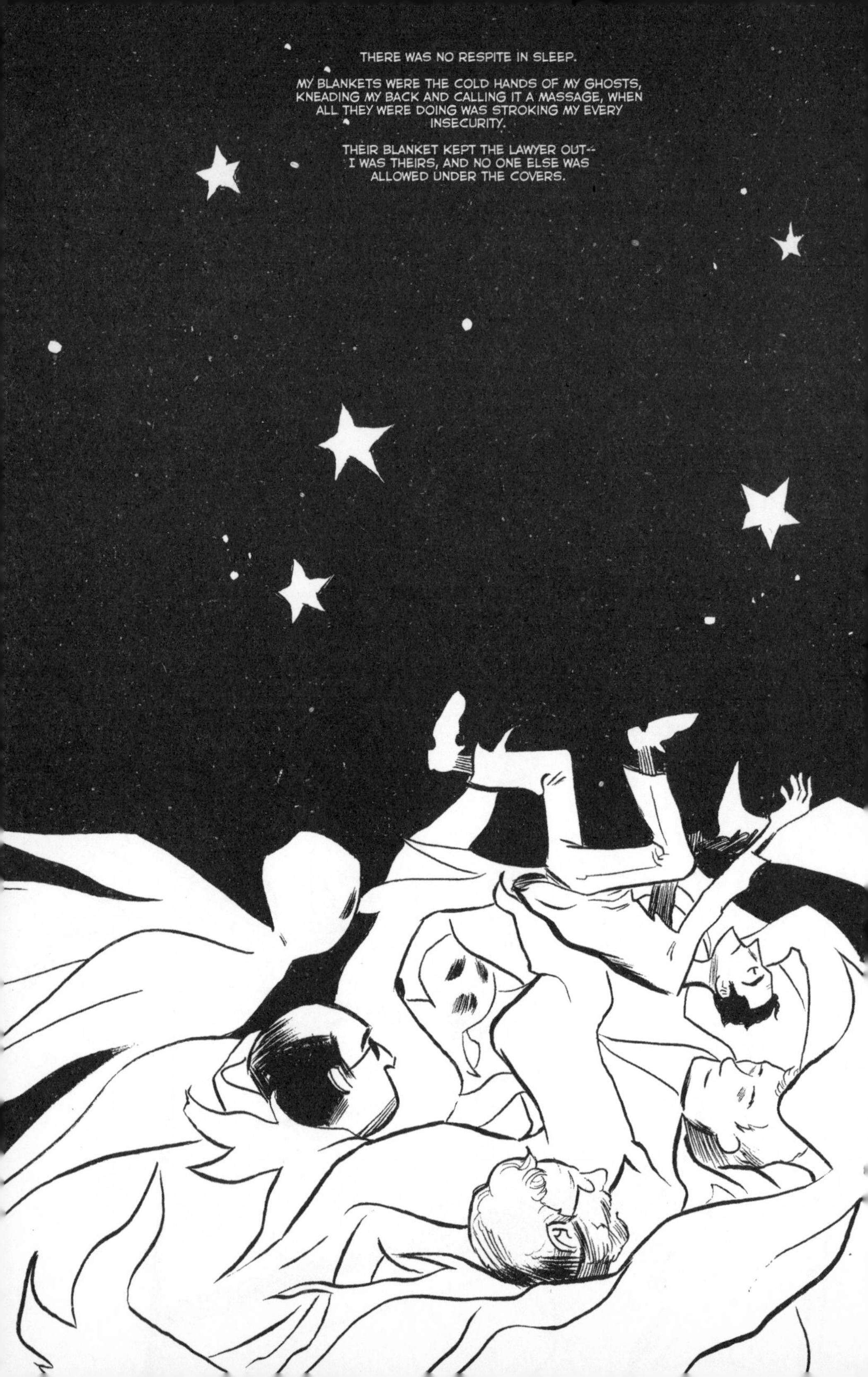
THERE WAS NO RESPITE IN SLEEP.
MY BLANKETS WERE THE COLD HANDS OF MY GHOSTS, KNEADING MY BACK AND CALLING IT A MASSAGE, WHEN ALL THEY WERE DOING WAS STROKING MY EVERY INSECURITY.
THEIR BLANKET KEPT THE LAWYER OUT-- I WAS THEIRS, AND NO ONE ELSE WAS ALLOWED UNDER THE COVERS.

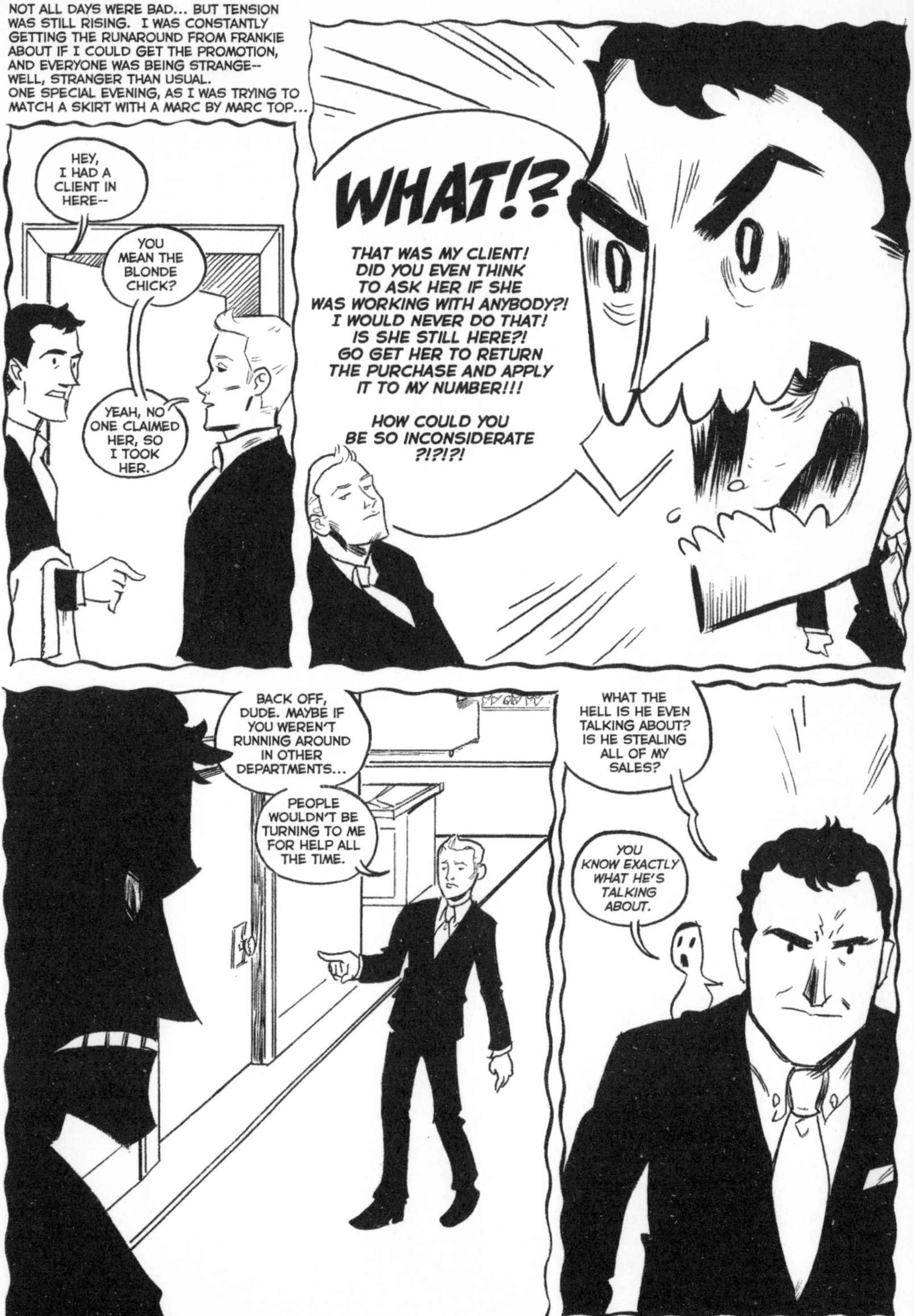
NOT ALL DAYS WERE BAD... BUT TENSION WAS STILL RISING. I WAS CONSTANTLY GETTING THE RUNAROUND FROM FRANKIE ABOUT IF I COULD GET THE PROMOTION, AND EVERYONE WAS BEING STRANGE-- WELL, STRANGER THAN USUAL.
ONE SPECIAL EVENING, AS I WAS TRYING TO MATCH A SKIRT WITH A MARC BY MARC TOP...
HEY, I HAD A CLIENT IN HERE--
YOU MEAN THE BLONDE CHICK?
YEAH, NO ONE CLAIMED HER, SO I TOOK HER.
WHAT!?
THAT WAS MY CLIENT! DID YOU EVEN THINK TO ASK HER IF SHE WAS WORKING WITH ANYBODY?! I WOULD NEVER DO THAT! IS SHE STILL HERE?! GO GET HER TO RETURN THE PURCHASE AND APPLY IT TO MY NUMBER!!!
HOW COULD YOU BE SO INCONSIDERATE ?!?!?!
BACK OFF, DUDE. MAYBE IF YOU WEREN'T RUNNING AROUND IN OTHER DEPARTMENTS...
PEOPLE WOULDN'T BE TURNING TO ME FOR HELP ALL THE TIME.
WHAT THE HELL IS HE EVEN TALKING ABOUT? IS HE STEALING ALL OF MY SALES?
YOU KNOW EXACTLY WHAT HE'S TALKING ABOUT.
IT WAS TRUE... THE SHOE GUY WASN'T TRYING TO SWOOP IN ON MY SALES... HE WAS TRYING TO GET THE PROMOTION.

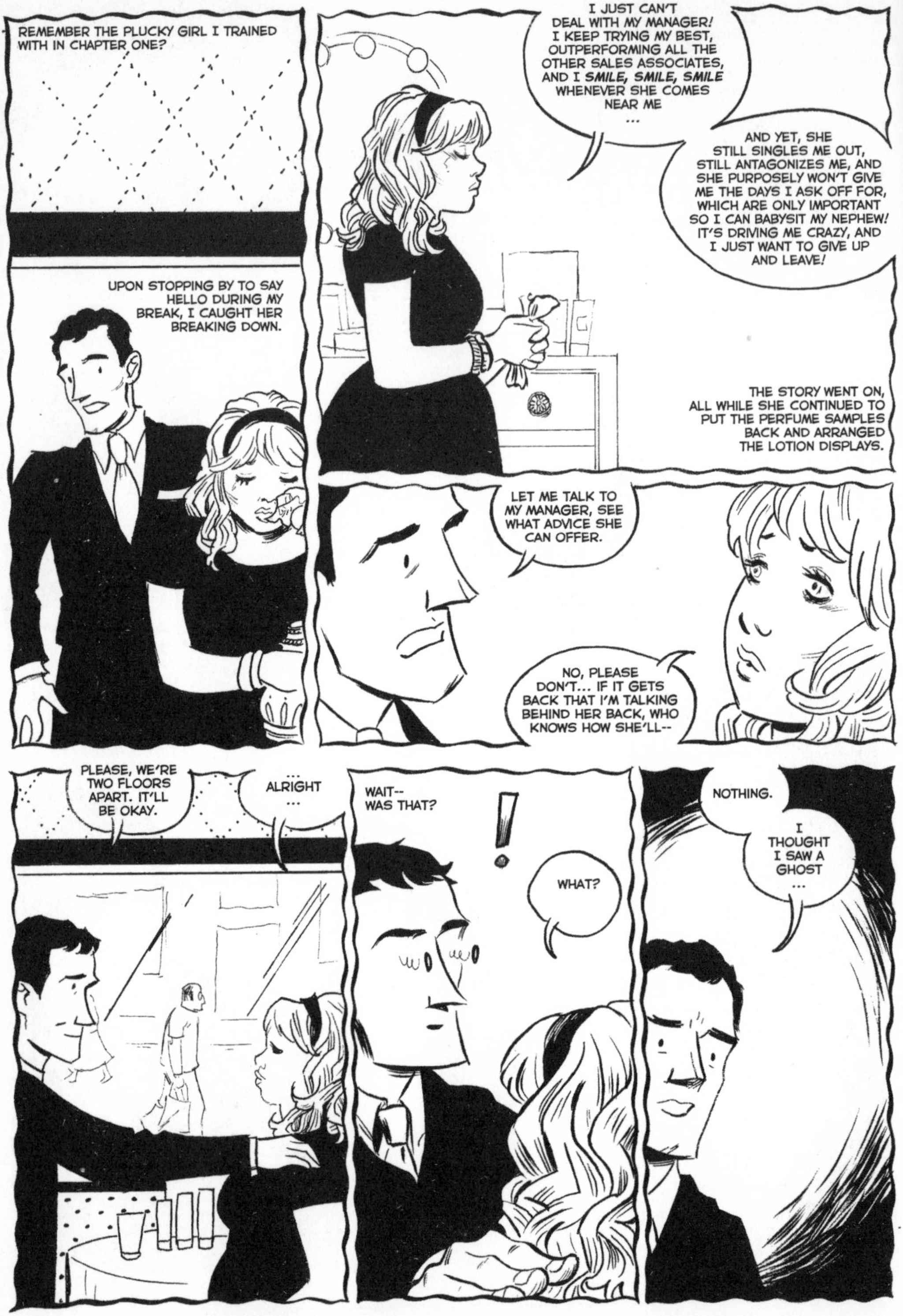
REMEMBER THE PLUCKY GIRL I TRAINED WITH IN CHAPTER ONE?
UPON STOPPING BY TO SAY HELLO DURING MY BREAK, I CAUGHT HER BREAKING DOWN.
I JUST CAN'T DEAL WITH MY MANAGER! I KEEP TRYING MY BEST, OUTPERFORMING ALL THE OTHER SALES ASSOCIATES, AND I SMILE, SMILE, SMILE WHENEVER SHE COMES NEAR ME ...
AND YET, SHE STILL SINGLES ME OUT, STILL ANTAGONIZES ME, AND SHE PURPOSELY WON'T GIVE ME THE DAYS I ASK OFF FOR, WHICH ARE ONLY IMPORTANT SO I CAN BABYSIT MY NEPHEW! IT'S DRIVING ME CRAZY, AND I JUST WANT TO GIVE UP AND LEAVE!
THE STORY WENT ON, ALL WHILE SHE CONTINUED TO PUT THE PERFUME SAMPLES BACK AND ARRANGED THE LOTION DISPLAYS.
LET ME TALK TO MY MANAGER, SEE WHAT ADVICE SHE CAN OFFER.
NO, PLEASE DON'T... IF IT GETS BACK THAT I'M TALKING BEHIND HER BACK, WHO KNOWS HOW SHE'LL--
PLEASE, WE'RE TWO FLOORS APART. IT'LL BE OKAY.
... ALRIGHT ...
WAIT-- WAS THAT?
!
WHAT?
NOTHING.
I THOUGHT I SAW A GHOST ...

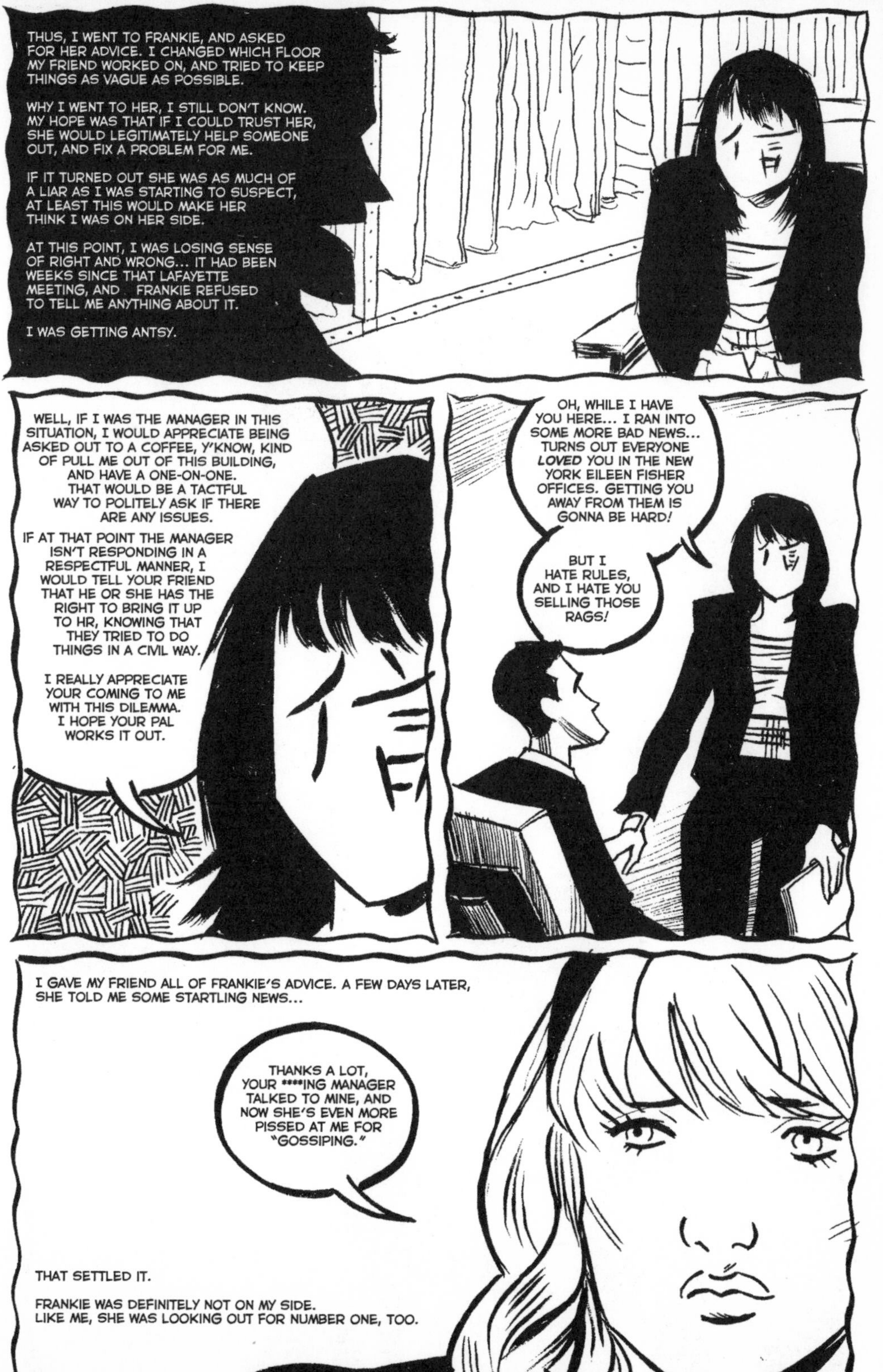
THUS, I WENT TO FRANKIE, AND ASKED FOR HER ADVICE. I CHANGED WHICH FLOOR MY FRIEND WORKED ON, AND TRIED TO KEEP THINGS AS VAGUE AS POSSIBLE.
WHY I WENT TO HER, I STILL DON'T KNOW. MY HOPE WAS THAT IF I COULD TRUST HER, SHE WOULD LEGITIMATELY HELP SOMEONE OUT, AND FIX A PROBLEM FOR ME.
IF IT TURNED OUT SHE WAS AS MUCH OF A LIAR AS I WAS STARTING TO SUSPECT, AT LEAST THIS WOULD MAKE HER THINK I WAS ON HER SIDE.
AT THIS POINT, I WAS LOSING SENSE OF RIGHT AND WRONG... IT HAD BEEN WEEKS SINCE THAT LAFAYETTE MEETING, AND FRANKIE REFUSED TO TELL ME ANYTHING ABOUT IT.
I WAS GETTING ANTSY.
WELL, IF I WAS THE MANAGER IN THIS SITUATION, I WOULD APPRECIATE BEING ASKED OUT TO A COFFEE, Y'KNOW, KIND OF PULL ME OUT OF THIS BUILDING, AND HAVE A ONE-ON-ONE. THAT WOULD BE A TACTFUL WAY TO POLITELY ASK IF THERE ARE ANY ISSUES.
IF AT THAT POINT THE MANAGER ISN'T RESPONDING IN A RESPECTFUL MANNER, I WOULD TELL YOUR FRIEND THAT HE OR SHE HAS THE RIGHT TO BRING IT UP TO HR, KNOWING THAT THEY TRIED TO DO THINGS IN A CIVIL WAY.
I REALLY APPRECIATE YOUR COMING TO ME WITH THIS DILEMMA. I HOPE YOUR PAL WORKS IT OUT.
OH, WHILE I HAVE YOU HERE... I RAN INTO SOME MORE BAD NEWS... TURNS OUT EVERYONE *LOVED* YOU IN THE NEW YORK EILEEN FISHER OFFICES. GETTING YOU AWAY FROM THEM IS GONNA BE HARD!
BUT I HATE RULES, AND I HATE YOU SELLING THOSE RAGS!
I GAVE MY FRIEND ALL OF FRANKIE'S ADVICE. A FEW DAYS LATER, SHE TOLD ME SOME STARTLING NEWS...
THANKS A LOT, YOUR ****ING MANAGER TALKED TO MINE, AND NOW SHE'S EVEN MORE PISSED AT ME FOR "GOSSIPING."
THAT SETTLED IT.
FRANKIE WAS DEFINITELY NOT ON MY SIDE. LIKE ME, SHE WAS LOOKING OUT FOR NUMBER ONE, TOO.

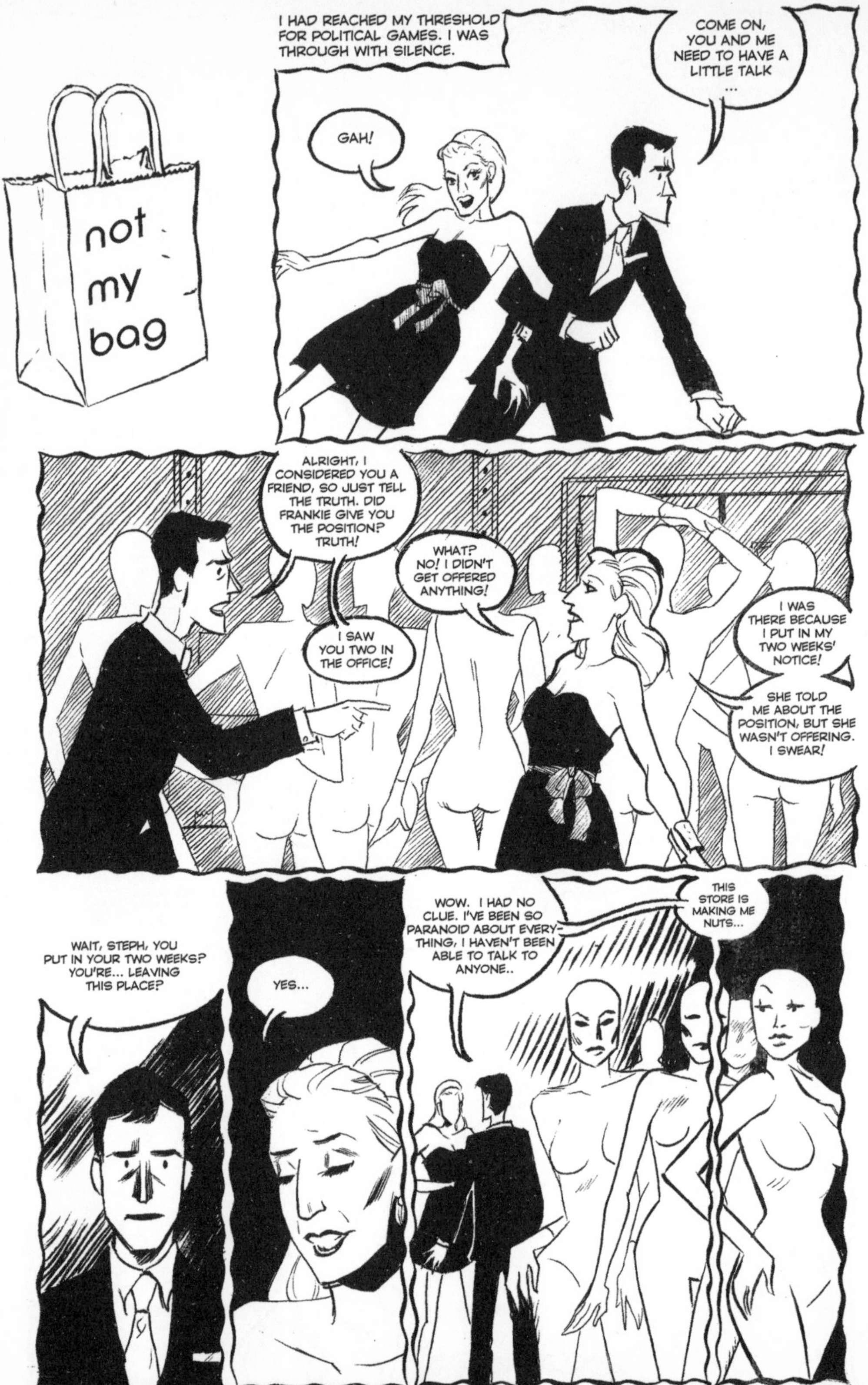

not my bag
I HAD REACHED MY THRESHOLD FOR POLITICAL GAMES. I WAS THROUGH WITH SILENCE.
COME ON, YOU AND ME NEED TO HAVE A LITTLE TALK ...
GAH!
ALRIGHT, I CONSIDERED YOU A FRIEND, SO JUST TELL THE TRUTH. DID FRANKIE GIVE YOU THE POSITION? TRUTH!
I SAW YOU TWO IN THE OFFICE!
WHAT? NO! I DIDN'T GET OFFERED ANYTHING!
I WAS THERE BECAUSE I PUT IN MY TWO WEEKS' NOTICE!
SHE TOLD ME ABOUT THE POSITION, BUT SHE WASN'T OFFERING. I SWEAR!
WAIT, STEPH, YOU PUT IN YOUR TWO WEEKS? YOU'RE... LEAVING THIS PLACE?
YES...
WOW. I HAD NO CLUE. I'VE BEEN SO PARANOID ABOUT EVERY-THING, I HAVEN'T BEEN ABLE TO TALK TO ANYONE..
THIS STORE IS MAKING ME NUTS...

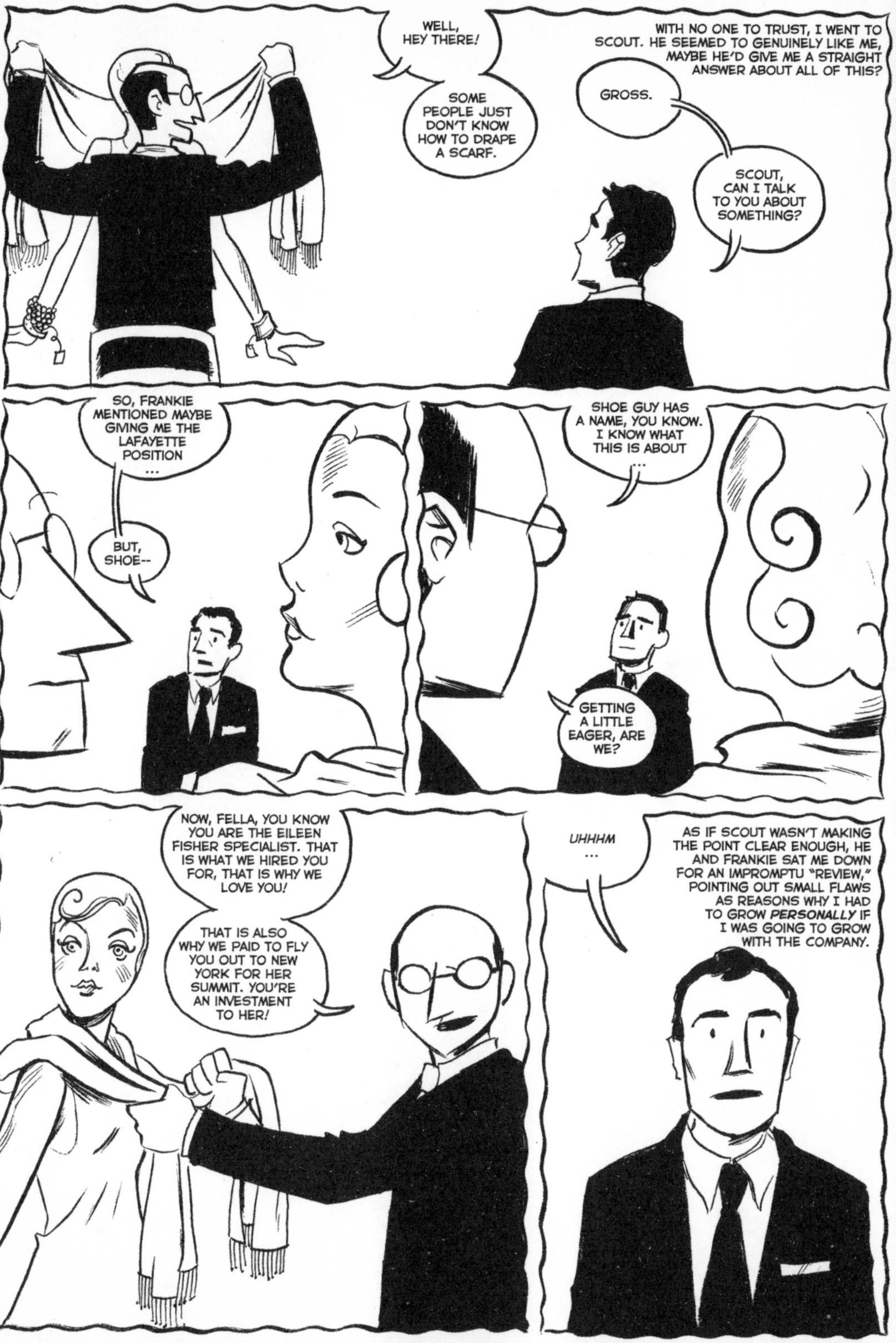
WELL, HEY THERE!
SOME PEOPLE JUST DON'T KNOW HOW TO DRAPE A SCARF.
WITH NO ONE TO TRUST, I WENT TO SCOUT. HE SEEMED TO GENUINELY LIKE ME, MAYBE HE'D GIVE ME A STRAIGHT ANSWER ABOUT ALL OF THIS?
GROSS.
SCOUT, CAN I TALK TO YOU ABOUT SOMETHING?
SO, FRANKIE MENTIONED MAYBE GIVING ME THE LAFAYETTE POSITION ...
BUT, SHOE--
SHOE GUY HAS A NAME, YOU KNOW. I KNOW WHAT THIS IS ABOUT ...
GETTING A LITTLE EAGER, ARE WE?
NOW, FELLA, YOU KNOW YOU ARE THE EILEEN FISHER SPECIALIST. THAT IS WHAT WE HIRED YOU FOR, THAT IS WHY WE LOVE YOU!
THAT IS ALSO WHY WE PAID TO FLY YOU OUT TO NEW YORK FOR HER SUMMIT. YOU'RE AN INVESTMENT TO HER!
UHHHM ...
AS IF SCOUT WASN'T MAKING THE POINT CLEAR ENOUGH, HE AND FRANKIE SAT ME DOWN FOR AN IMPROMPTU "REVIEW," POINTING OUT SMALL FLAWS AS REASONS WHY I HAD TO GROW PERSONALLY IF I WAS GOING TO GROW WITH THE COMPANY.

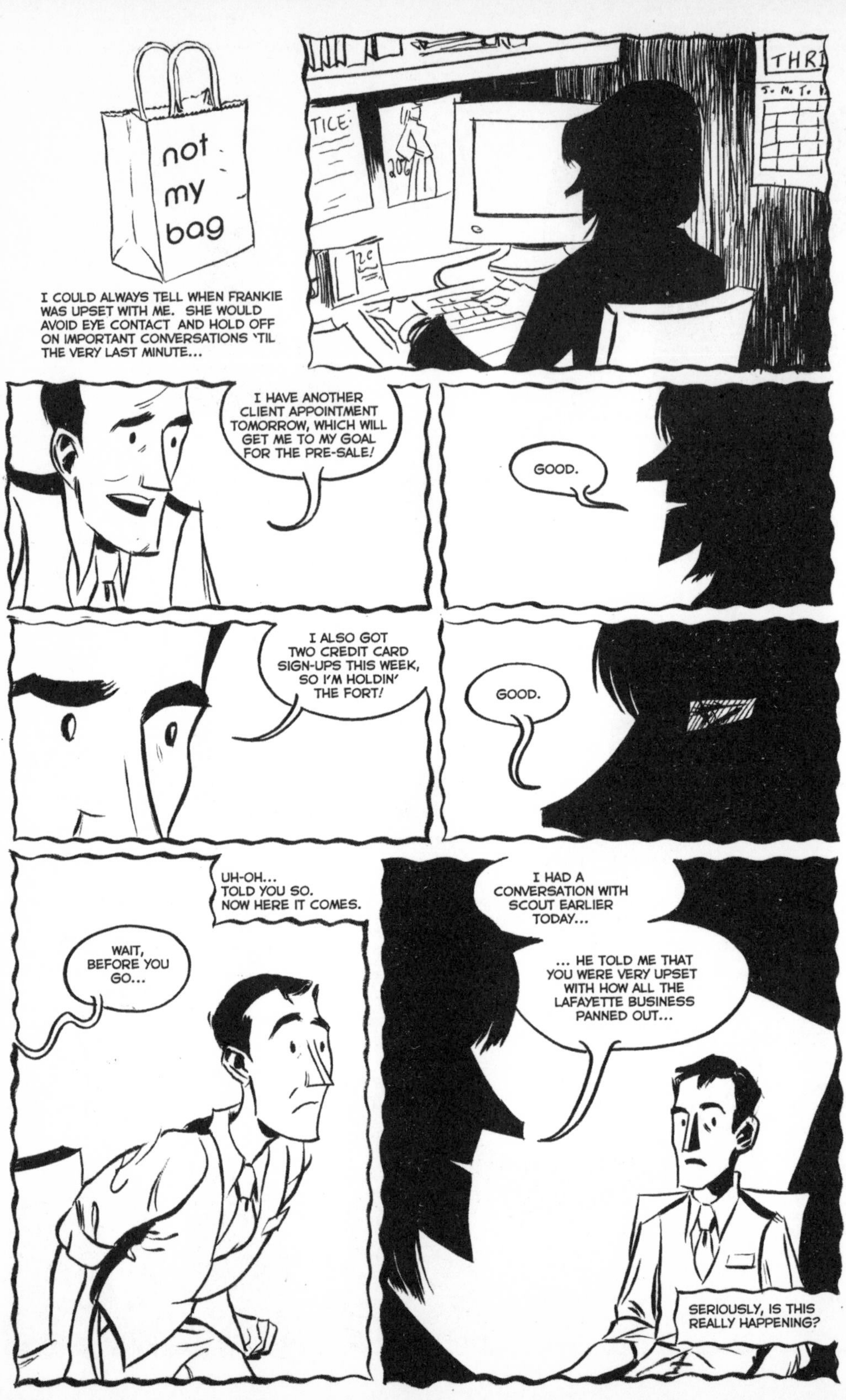
not my bag
I COULD ALWAYS TELL WHEN FRANKIE WAS UPSET WITH ME. SHE WOULD AVOID EYE CONTACT AND HOLD OFF ON IMPORTANT CONVERSATIONS 'TIL THE VERY LAST MINUTE...
THR
I HAVE ANOTHER CLIENT APPOINTMENT TOMORROW, WHICH WILL GET ME TO MY GOAL FOR THE PRE-SALE!
GOOD.
I ALSO GOT TWO CREDIT CARD SIGN-UPS THIS WEEK, SO I'M HOLDIN' THE FORT!
GOOD.
UH-OH... TOLD YOU SO. NOW HERE IT COMES.
WAIT, BEFORE YOU GO...
I HAD A CONVERSATION WITH SCOUT EARLIER TODAY...
... HE TOLD ME THAT YOU WERE VERY UPSET WITH HOW ALL THE LAFAYETTE BUSINESS PANNED OUT...
SERIOUSLY, IS THIS REALLY HAPPENING?

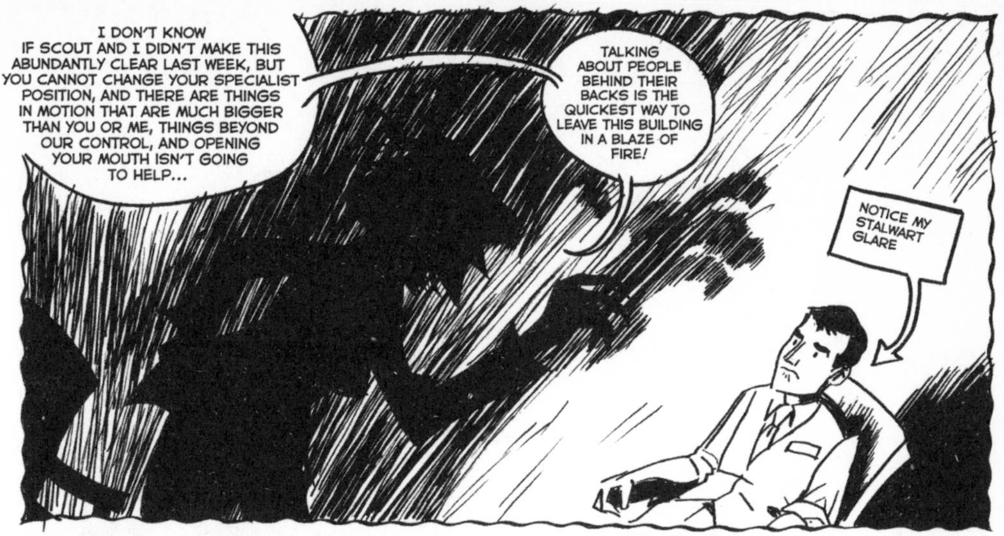
I DON'T KNOW IF SCOUT AND I DIDN'T MAKE THIS ABUNDANTLY CLEAR LAST WEEK, BUT YOU CANNOT CHANGE YOUR SPECIALIST POSITION, AND THERE ARE THINGS IN MOTION THAT ARE MUCH BIGGER THAN YOU OR ME, THINGS BEYOND OUR CONTROL, AND OPENING YOUR MOUTH ISN'T GOING TO HELP...
TALKING ABOUT PEOPLE BEHIND THEIR BACKS IS THE QUICKEST WAY TO LEAVE THIS BUILDING IN A BLAZE OF FIRE!
NOTICE MY STALWART GLARE

THERE ARE MOMENTS IN YOUR LIFE WHERE YOU GET INCREDIBLY TIRED OF WATCHING OTHERS FLAUNT THEIR POWER AND GO ON ABOUT YOUR INSIGNIFICANCE.

WHEN I WAS YOUNGER, I NEVER HAD A SNAPPY COMEBACK IN TIME, AND AS I GOT OLDER, I THEN BECAME TOO TIMID TO ACTUALLY BITE BACK.

AT THAT VERY MOMENT, HOWEVER, I WAS SO DONE WITH HOLDING BACK, WITH SILENCE, AND DELIBERATION...

I DIDN'T NEED THIS WOMAN FOR ANYTHING. SHE WOULD NEVER BE USED AS A REFERENCE, AND WOULD ONLY BE DOING A FAVOR BY FIRING ME.

FRANKIE WANTED TO FIGHT WITH GLOVES OFF? BRING IT.

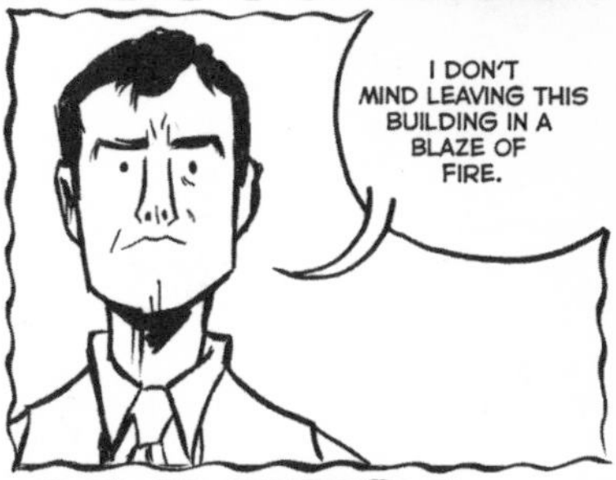
I DON'T MIND LEAVING THIS BUILDING IN A BLAZE OF FIRE.

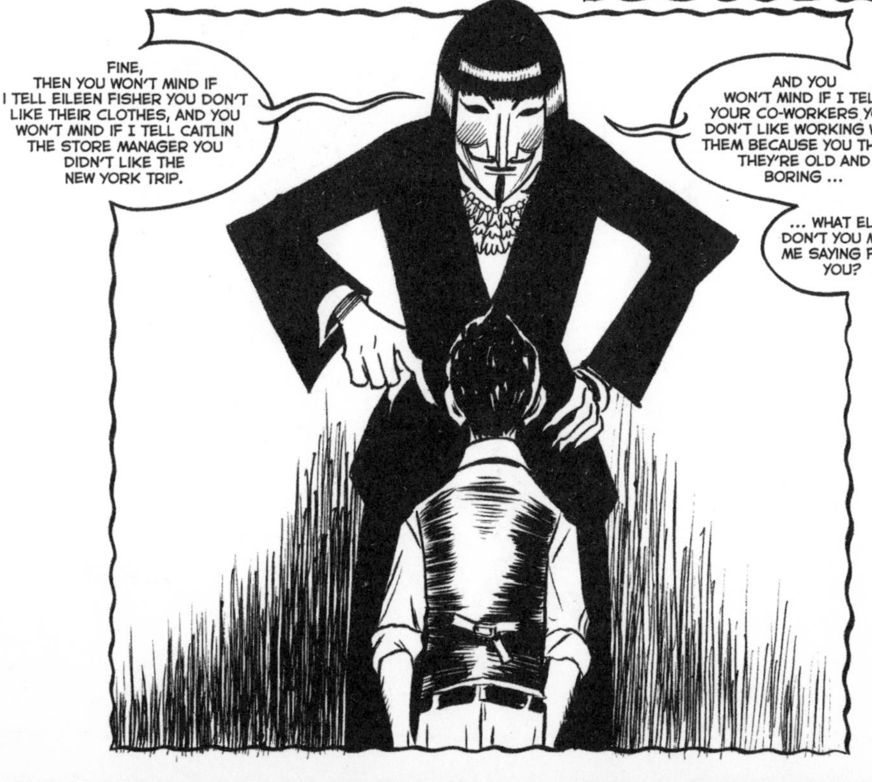
FINE, THEN YOU WON'T MIND IF I TELL EILEEN FISHER YOU DON'T LIKE THEIR CLOTHES, AND YOU WON'T MIND IF I TELL CAITLIN THE STORE MANAGER YOU DIDN'T LIKE THE NEW YORK TRIP.
AND YOU WON'T MIND IF I TELL YOUR CO-WORKERS YOU DON'T LIKE WORKING WITH THEM BECAUSE YOU THINK THEY'RE OLD AND BORING ...
... WHAT ELSE DON'T YOU MIND ME SAYING FOR YOU?

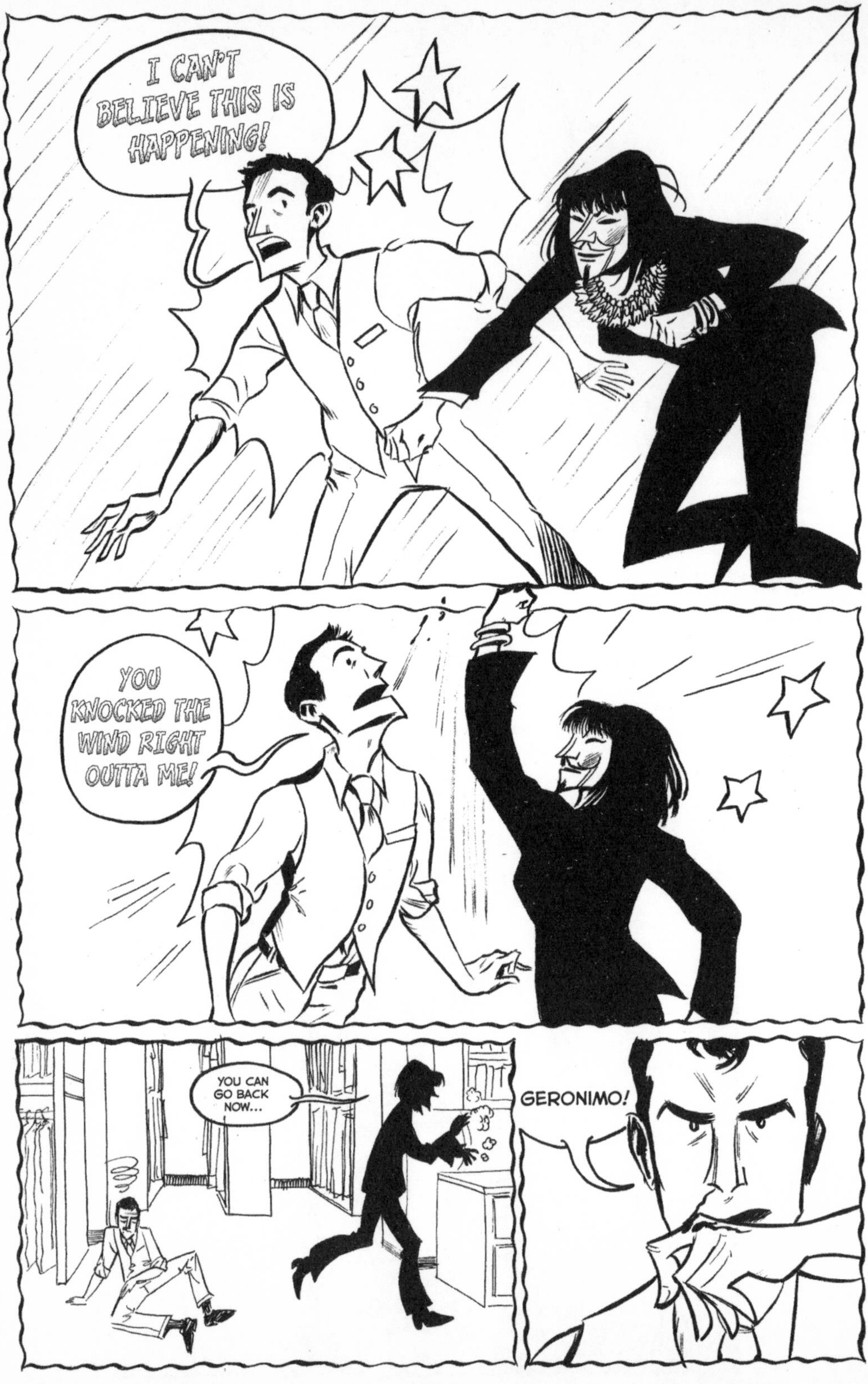
I CAN'T BELIEVE THIS IS HAPPENING!
YOU KNOCKED THE WIND RIGHT OUTTA ME!
YOU CAN GO BACK NOW...
GERONIMO!

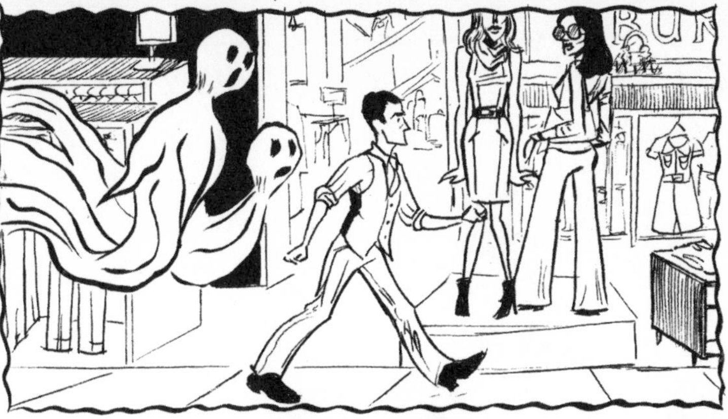

MY CAR INSURANCE WAS PAID OFF, I HAD ENOUGH SAVED UP THAT I COULD BE WITHOUT A JOB.

LIFE DIDN'T FEEL LIKE IT WAS IN MY CONTROL, AND I HAD TO CHANGE THAT.

NO MORE GHOSTS, NO MORE MASKS.

THIS BAD BUSINESS WAS BEYOND DUMB.

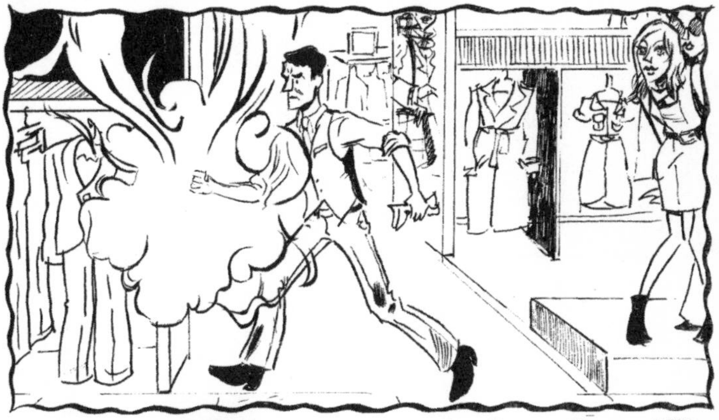

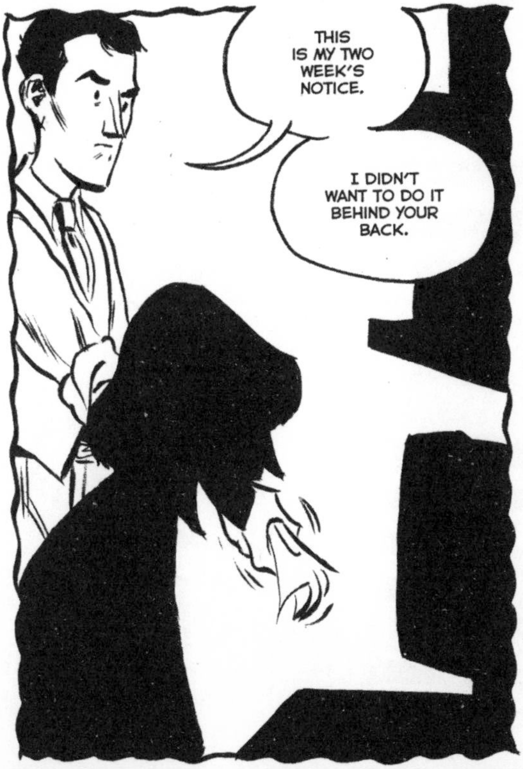
THIS IS MY TWO WEEK'S NOTICE.
I DIDN'T WANT TO DO IT BEHIND YOUR BACK.

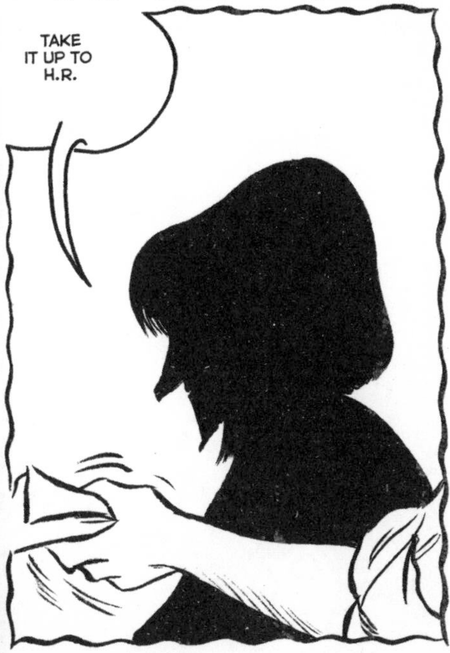
TAKE IT UP TO H.R.

MY HAND COULDN'T STOP SHAKING. EVEN WITH A MASK ON, FRANKIE KEPT HER FACE TURNED AWAY FROM ME.

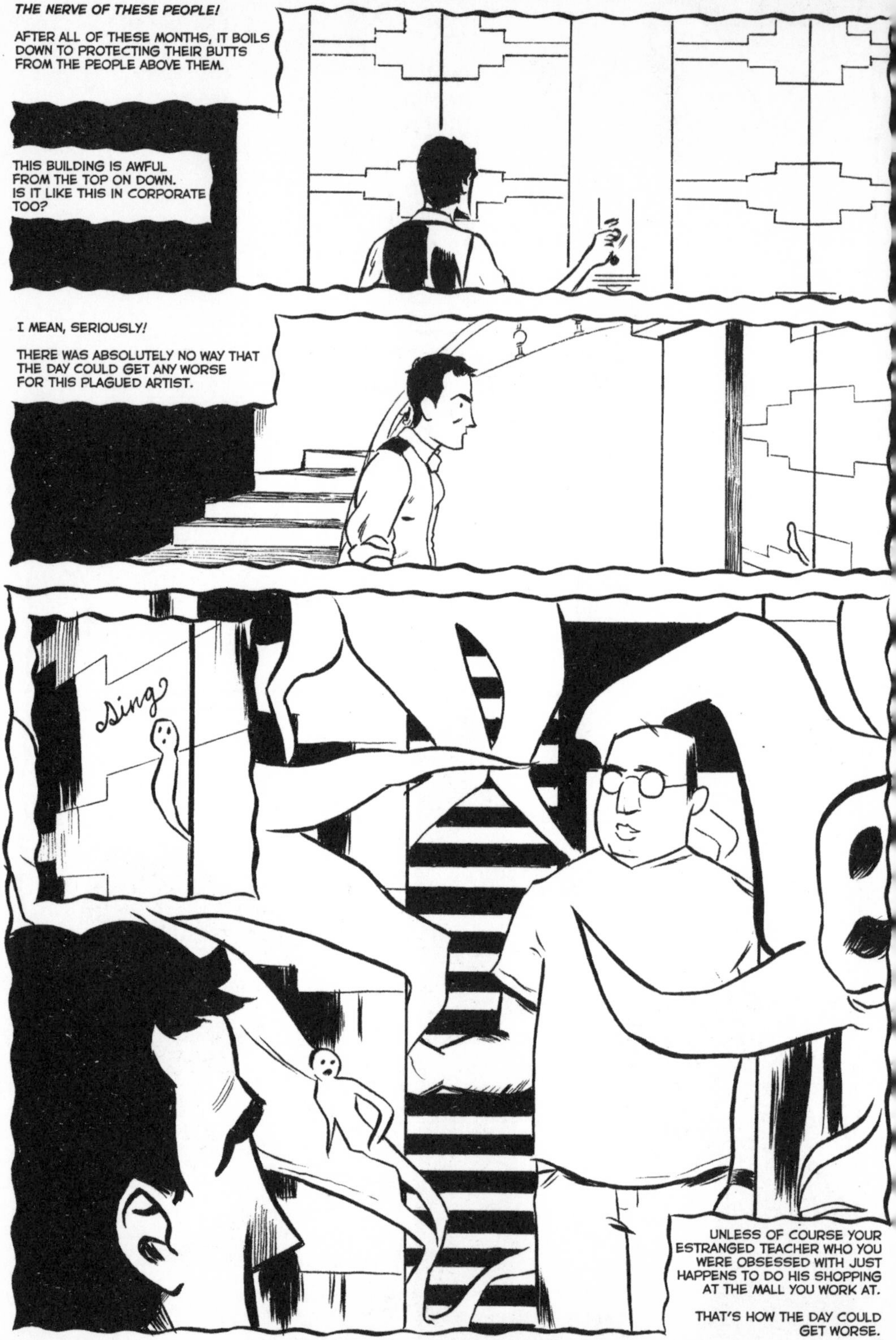

THE NERVE OF THESE PEOPLE!
AFTER ALL OF THESE MONTHS, IT BOILS DOWN TO PROTECTING THEIR BUTTS FROM THE PEOPLE ABOVE THEM.
THIS BUILDING IS AWFUL FROM THE TOP ON DOWN. IS IT LIKE THIS IN CORPORATE TOO?
I MEAN, SERIOUSLY!
THERE WAS ABSOLUTELY NO WAY THAT THE DAY COULD GET ANY WORSE FOR THIS PLAGUED ARTIST.
Ding
UNLESS OF COURSE YOUR ESTRANGED TEACHER WHO YOU WERE OBSESSED WITH JUST HAPPENS TO DO HIS SHOPPING AT THE MALL YOU WORK AT.
THAT'S HOW THE DAY COULD GET WORSE.

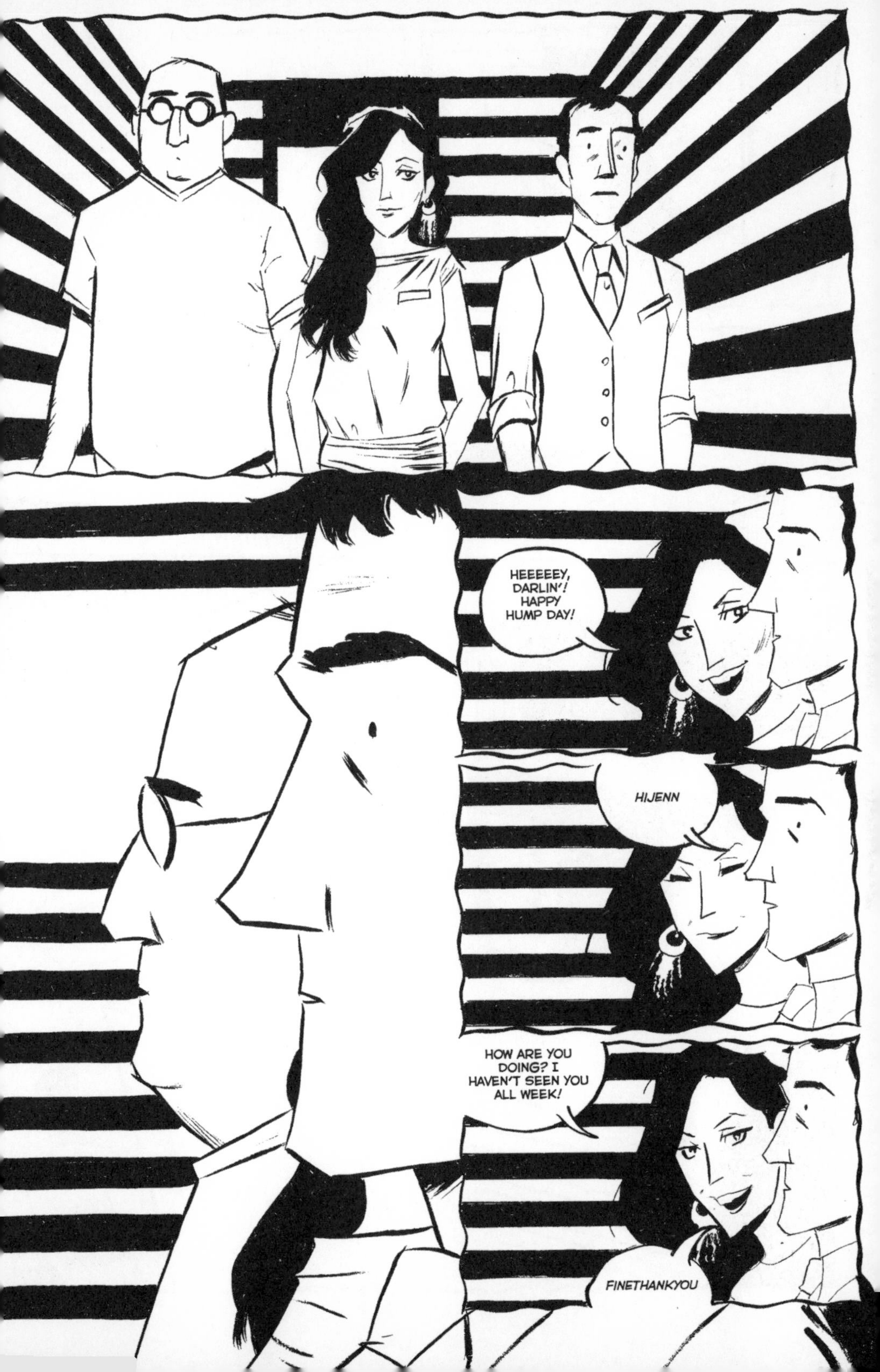
HEEEEEY, DARLIN'! HAPPY HUMP DAY!
HIJENN
HOW ARE YOU DOING? I HAVEN'T SEEN YOU ALL WEEK!
FINETHANKYOU

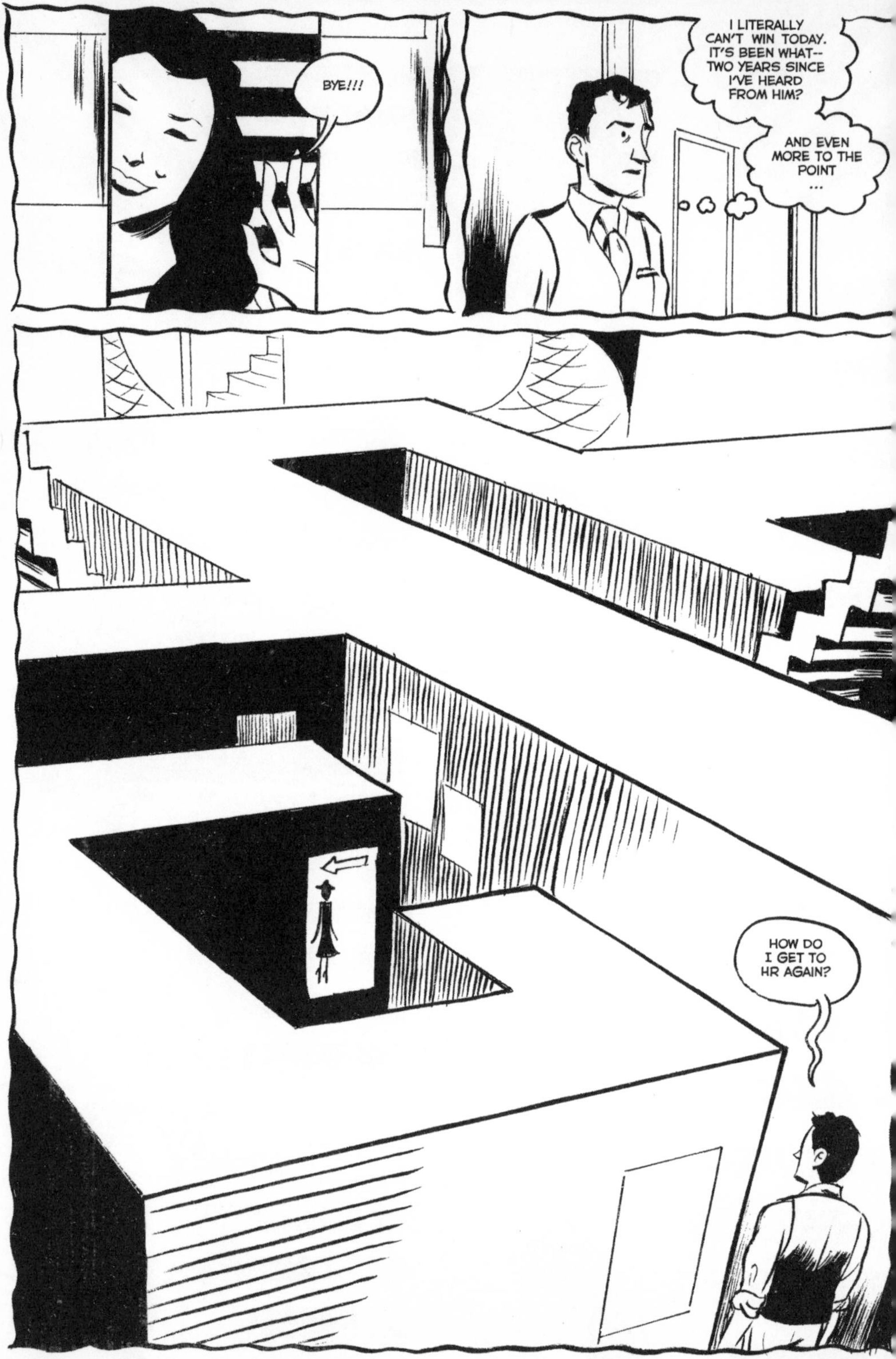

BYE!!!
I LITERALLY CAN'T WIN TODAY. IT'S BEEN WHAT-- TWO YEARS SINCE I'VE HEARD FROM HIM?
AND EVEN MORE TO THE POINT ...
HOW DO I GET TO HR AGAIN?

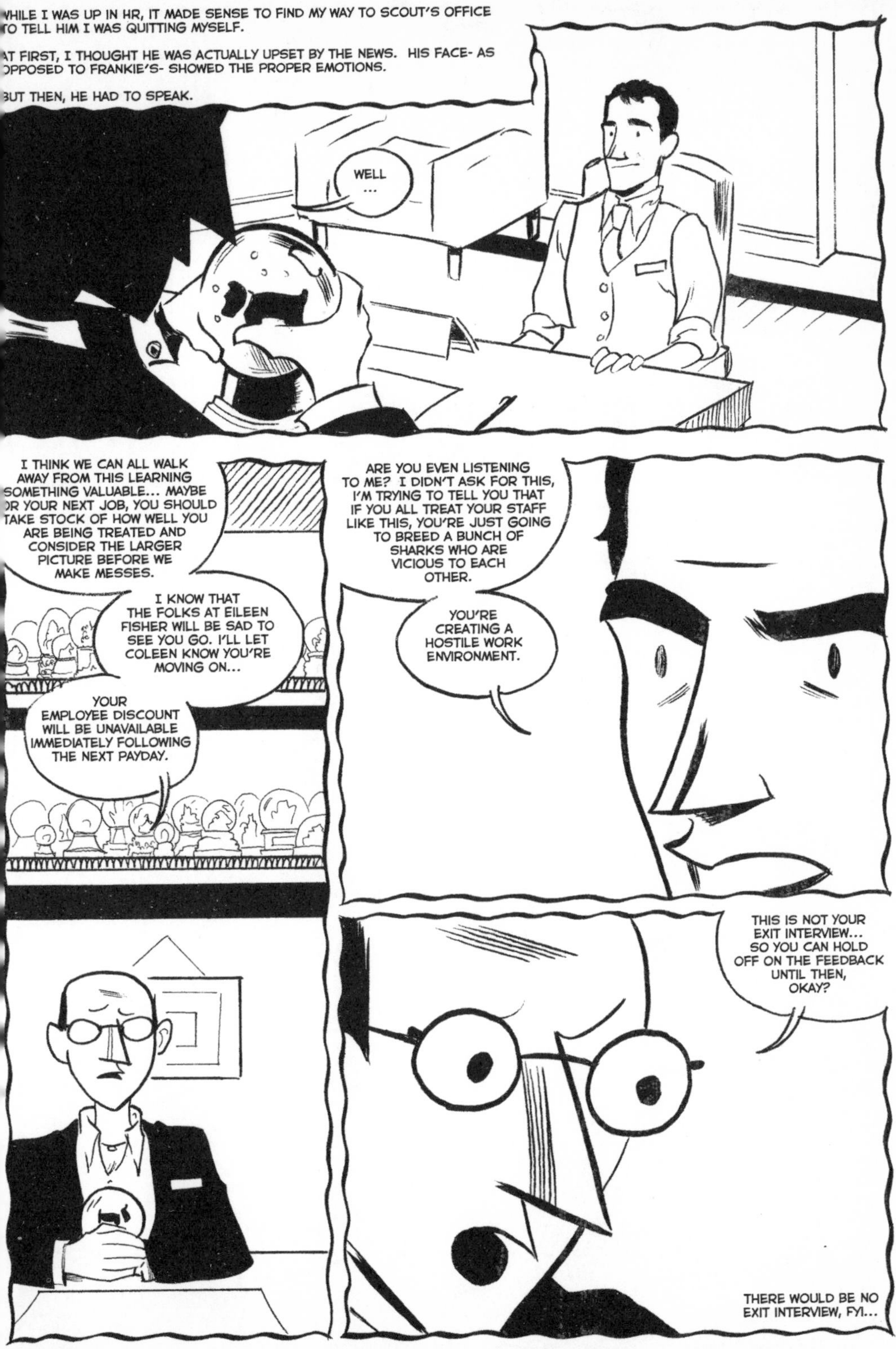
WHILE I WAS UP IN HR, IT MADE SENSE TO FIND MY WAY TO SCOUT'S OFFICE TO TELL HIM I WAS QUITTING MYSELF.
AT FIRST, I THOUGHT HE WAS ACTUALLY UPSET BY THE NEWS. HIS FACE- AS OPPOSED TO FRANKIE'S- SHOWED THE PROPER EMOTIONS.
BUT THEN, HE HAD TO SPEAK.
WELL ...
I THINK WE CAN ALL WALK AWAY FROM THIS LEARNING SOMETHING VALUABLE... MAYBE FOR YOUR NEXT JOB, YOU SHOULD TAKE STOCK OF HOW WELL YOU ARE BEING TREATED AND CONSIDER THE LARGER PICTURE BEFORE WE MAKE MESSES.
I KNOW THAT THE FOLKS AT EILEEN FISHER WILL BE SAD TO SEE YOU GO. I'LL LET COLEEN KNOW YOU'RE MOVING ON...
YOUR EMPLOYEE DISCOUNT WILL BE UNAVAILABLE IMMEDIATELY FOLLOWING THE NEXT PAYDAY.
ARE YOU EVEN LISTENING TO ME? I DIDN'T ASK FOR THIS, I'M TRYING TO TELL YOU THAT IF YOU ALL TREAT YOUR STAFF LIKE THIS, YOU'RE JUST GOING TO BREED A BUNCH OF SHARKS WHO ARE VICIOUS TO EACH OTHER.
YOU'RE CREATING A HOSTILE WORK ENVIRONMENT.
THIS IS NOT YOUR EXIT INTERVIEW... SO YOU CAN HOLD OFF ON THE FEEDBACK UNTIL THEN, OKAY?
THERE WOULD BE NO EXIT INTERVIEW, FYI...

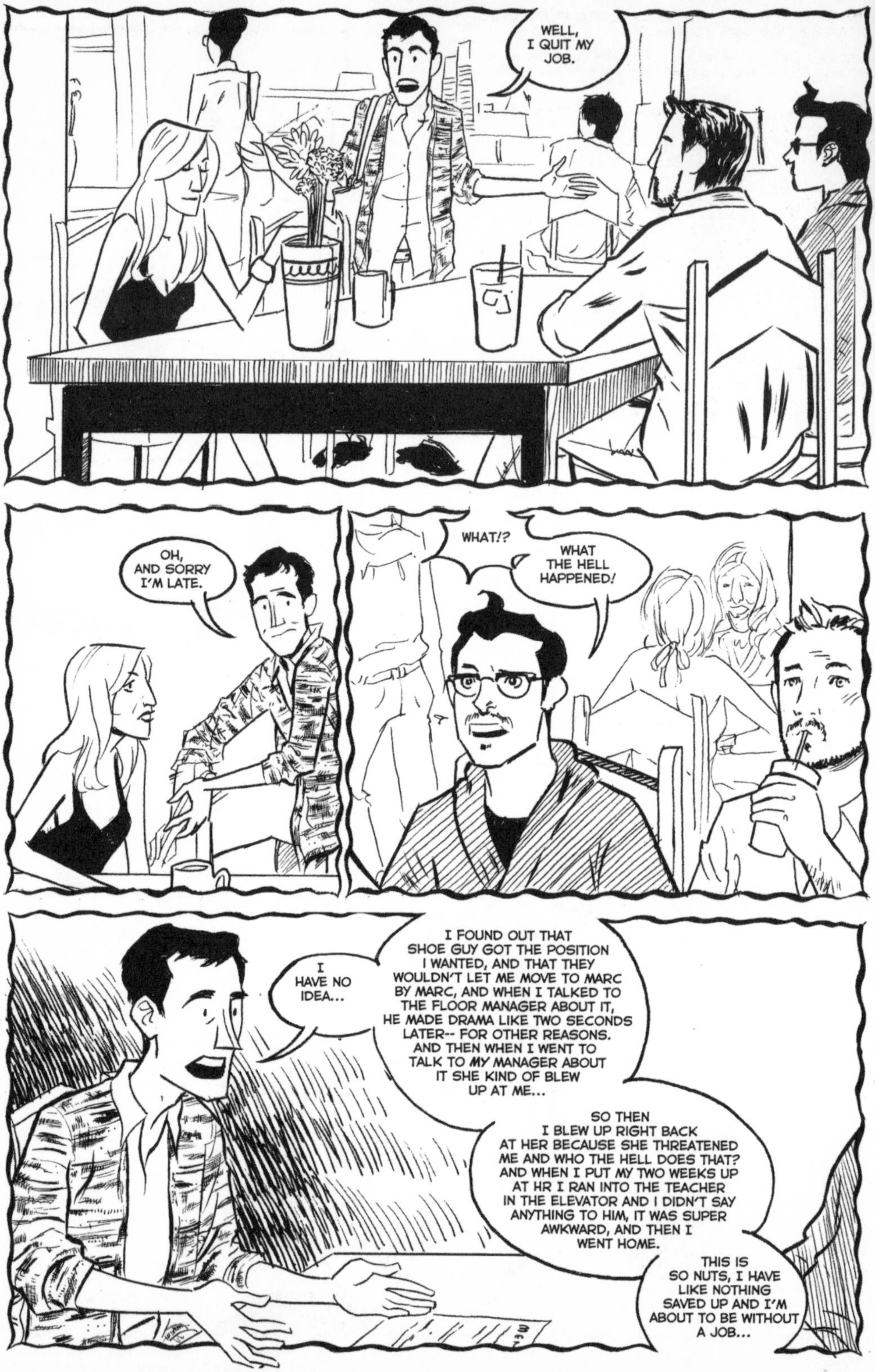

WELL, I QUIT MY JOB.
OH, AND SORRY I'M LATE.
WHAT!?
WHAT THE HELL HAPPENED!
I HAVE NO IDEA...
I FOUND OUT THAT SHOE GUY GOT THE POSITION I WANTED, AND THAT THEY WOULDN'T LET ME MOVE TO *MARC BY MARC*, AND WHEN I TALKED TO THE FLOOR MANAGER ABOUT IT, HE MADE DRAMA LIKE TWO SECONDS LATER-- FOR OTHER REASONS. AND THEN WHEN I WENT TO TALK TO *MY* MANAGER ABOUT IT SHE KIND OF BLEW UP AT ME...
SO THEN I BLEW UP RIGHT BACK AT HER BECAUSE SHE THREATENED ME AND WHO THE HELL DOES THAT? AND WHEN I PUT MY TWO WEEKS UP AT HR I RAN INTO THE TEACHER IN THE ELEVATOR AND I DIDN'T SAY ANYTHING TO HIM, IT WAS SUPER AWKWARD, AND THEN I WENT HOME.
THIS IS SO NUTS, I HAVE LIKE NOTHING SAVED UP AND I'M ABOUT TO BE WITHOUT A JOB...

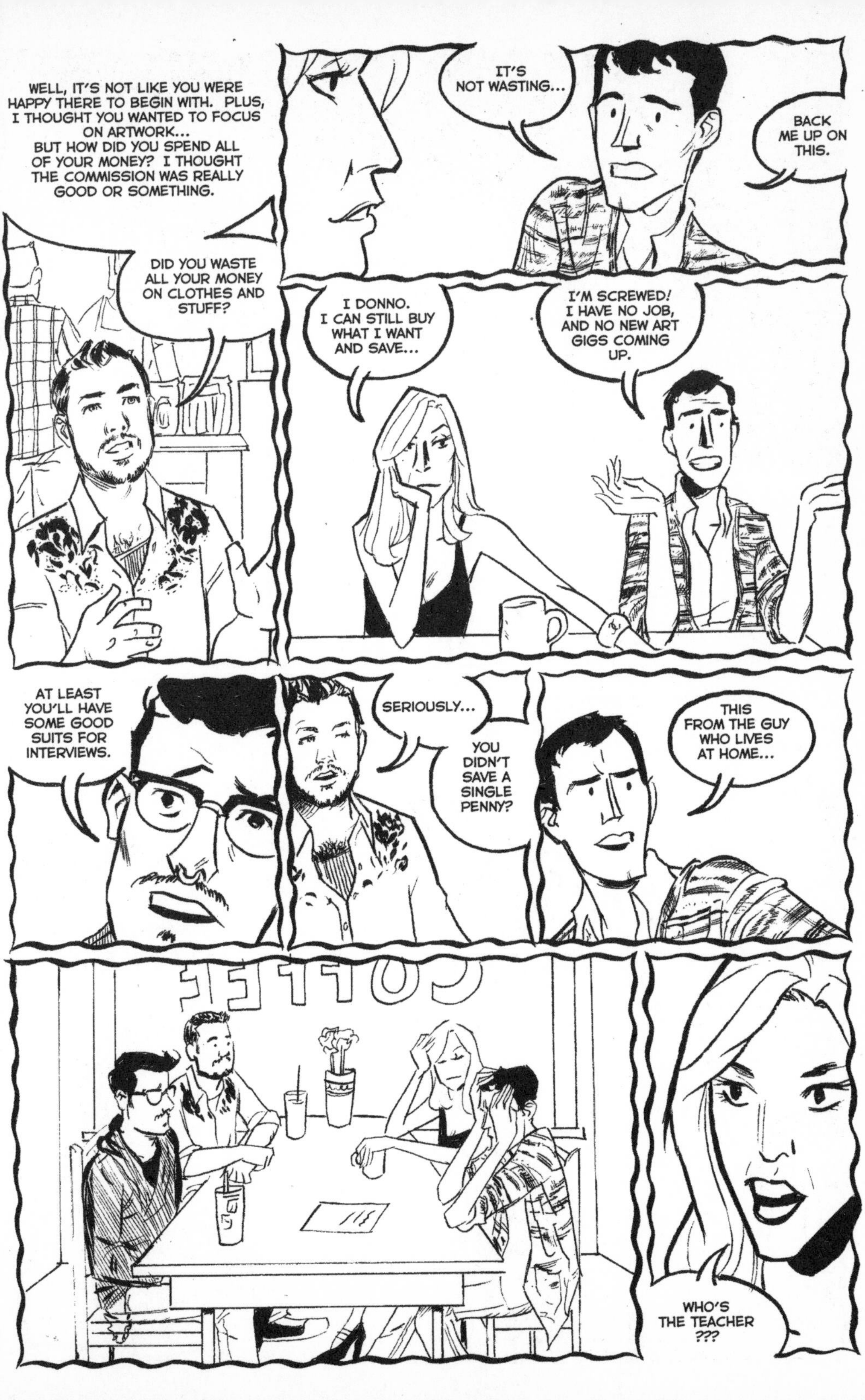
WELL, IT'S NOT LIKE YOU WERE HAPPY THERE TO BEGIN WITH. PLUS, I THOUGHT YOU WANTED TO FOCUS ON ARTWORK... BUT HOW DID YOU SPEND ALL OF YOUR MONEY? I THOUGHT THE COMMISSION WAS REALLY GOOD OR SOMETHING.
IT'S NOT WASTING...
BACK ME UP ON THIS.
DID YOU WASTE ALL YOUR MONEY ON CLOTHES AND STUFF?
I DONNO. I CAN STILL BUY WHAT I WANT AND SAVE...
I'M SCREWED! I HAVE NO JOB, AND NO NEW ART GIGS COMING UP.
AT LEAST YOU'LL HAVE SOME GOOD SUITS FOR INTERVIEWS.
SERIOUSLY...
YOU DIDN'T SAVE A SINGLE PENNY?
THIS FROM THE GUY WHO LIVES AT HOME...
COFFEE
WHO'S THE TEACHER ???

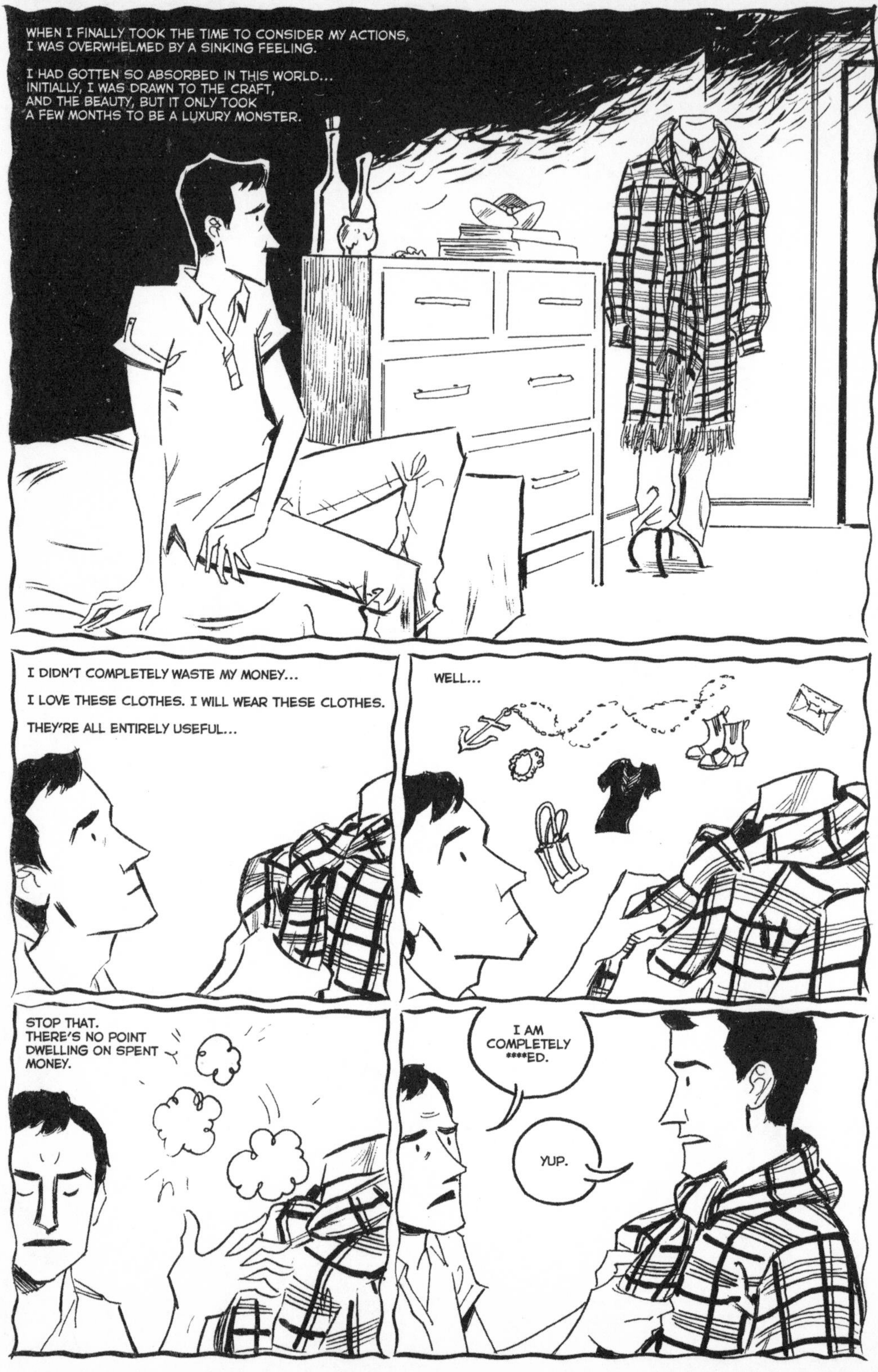
WHEN I FINALLY TOOK THE TIME TO CONSIDER MY ACTIONS, I WAS OVERWHELMED BY A SINKING FEELING.
I HAD GOTTEN SO ABSORBED IN THIS WORLD... INITIALLY, I WAS DRAWN TO THE CRAFT, AND THE BEAUTY, BUT IT ONLY TOOK A FEW MONTHS TO BE A LUXURY MONSTER.
I DIDN'T COMPLETELY WASTE MY MONEY...
I LOVE THESE CLOTHES. I WILL WEAR THESE CLOTHES.
THEY'RE ALL ENTIRELY USEFUL...
WELL...
STOP THAT. THERE'S NO POINT DWELLING ON SPENT MONEY.
I AM COMPLETELY ****ED.
YUP.

chapter
four

"True love does have the power to redeem but only if we are ready for redemption. Love saves us only if we want to be saved."

--bell hooks

IN LIFE, THERE IS A SIMPLE LESSON EVERY YOUNG, IMPRESSIONABLE WRITER - OR ARTIST - GOING OUT TO THE WORK FORCE SHOULD KNOW: THEY ARE NOT CARRIE BRADSHAW. THERE IS NO SUCH GLAMOUR FOR PEOPLE WHO WRITE. HIGH END RETAIL STORES ARE RATHER RETICENT TO LEND THEIR CLOTHES TO UP AND COMERS WHOSE FACES NEVER GRACE MAGAZINES, AND MOST IMPORTANTLY: THE FASHION IS REALLY ****ING EXPENSIVE.

AS MUCH AS I WANTED TO FALL INTO THAT WORLD, AND BECOME THAT SORT OF CARE-FREE CREATOR, IT WAS NOT HAPPENING. THE TERMS POP CULTURE SET FOR THEIR CHARACTERS WERE PROVING 100% UNFEASIBLE, THE DEPARTMENT STORE ALMOST DESTROYED ME, AND MY OWN DELUSIONS OF GRANDEUR ALMOST MADE ME GO BANKRUPT.

ON TOP OF THAT, THE CONSTANT OVER-ANALYZATION OF LOVE AND RELATIONSHIPS ALMOST KILLED MY CHANCES OF FINDING A RELATIONSHIP WORTH HAVING.

BUT, AS THE SAYING GOES:
KEEP CALM
AND
CARRIE ON.

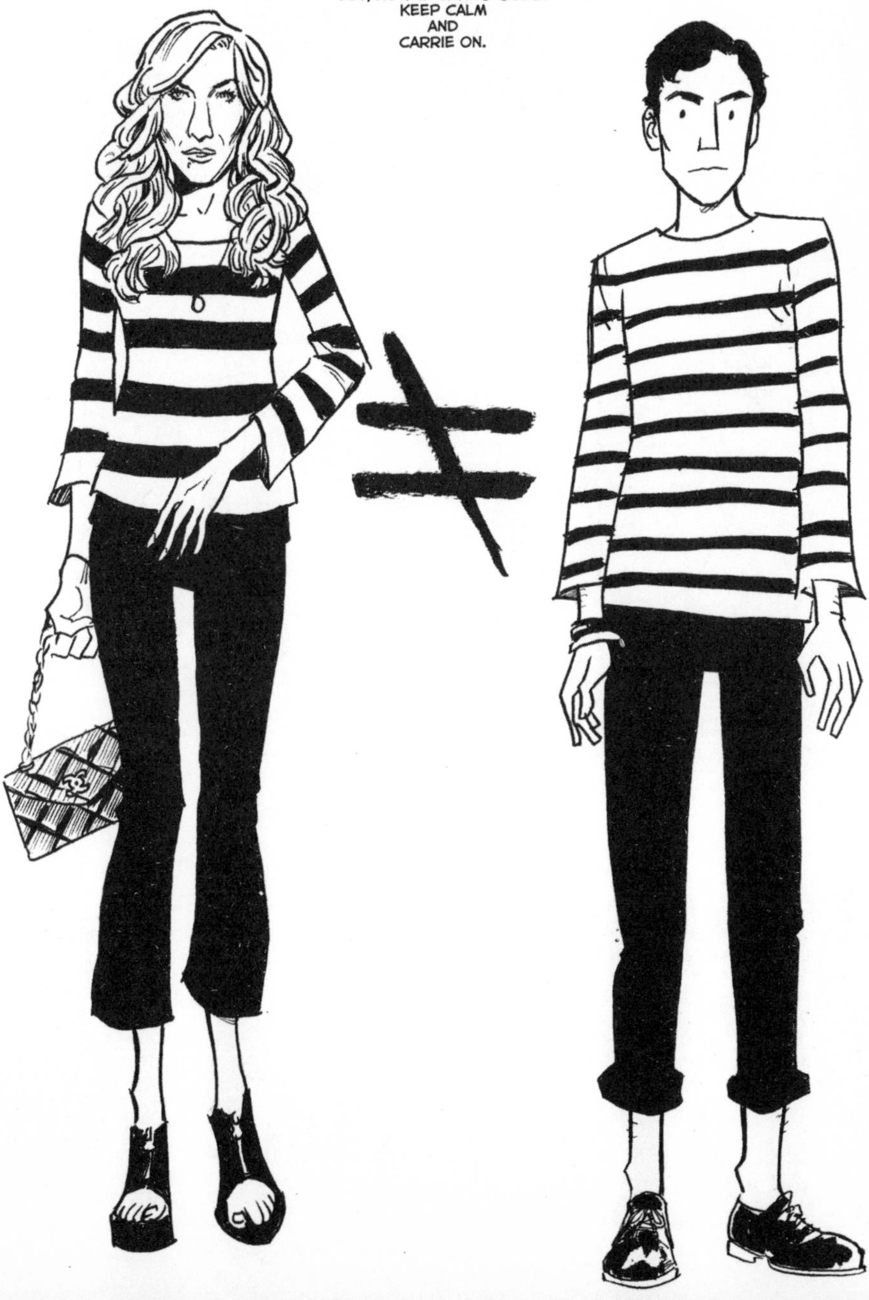

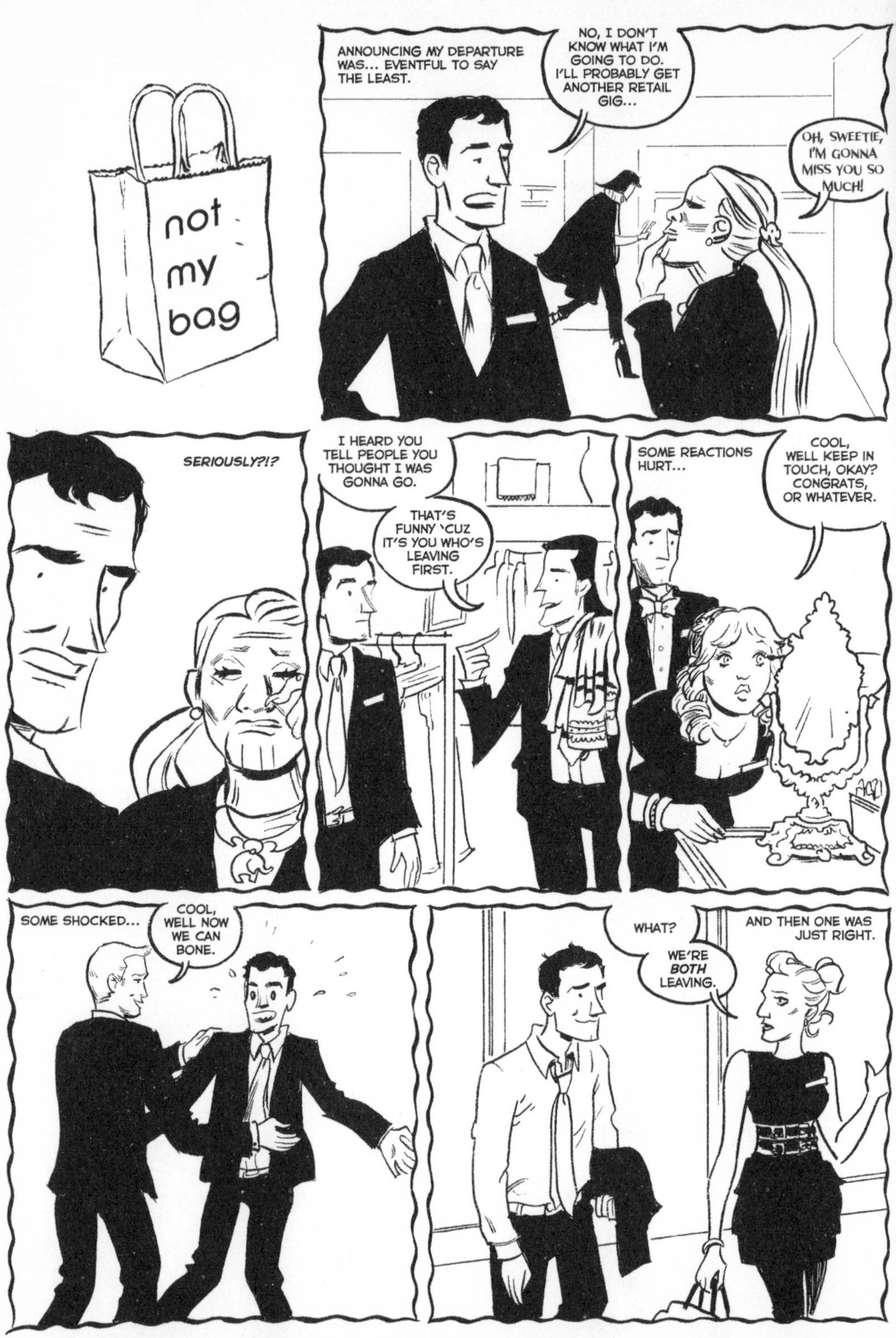
not my bag
ANNOUNCING MY DEPARTURE WAS... EVENTFUL TO SAY THE LEAST.
NO, I DON'T KNOW WHAT I'M GOING TO DO. I'LL PROBABLY GET ANOTHER RETAIL GIG...
OH, SWEETIE, I'M GONNA MISS YOU SO MUCH!
SERIOUSLY?!?
I HEARD YOU TELL PEOPLE YOU THOUGHT I WAS GONNA GO.
THAT'S FUNNY 'CUZ IT'S YOU WHO'S LEAVING FIRST.
SOME REACTIONS HURT...
COOL, WELL KEEP IN TOUCH, OKAY? CONGRATS, OR WHATEVER.
SOME SHOCKED...
COOL, WELL NOW WE CAN BONE.
AND THEN ONE WAS JUST RIGHT.
WHAT?
WE'RE *BOTH* LEAVING.

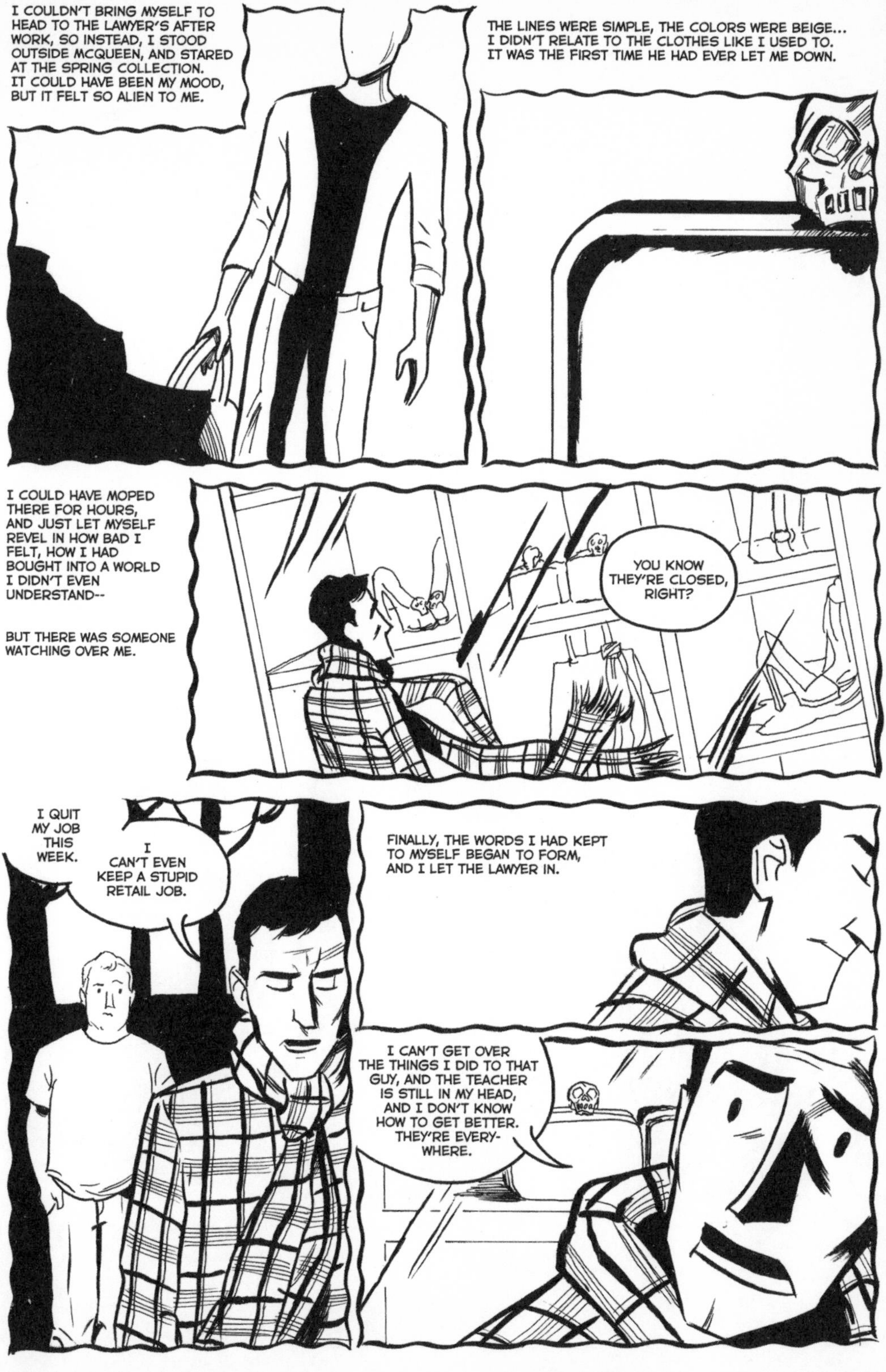
I COULDN'T BRING MYSELF TO HEAD TO THE LAWYER'S AFTER WORK, SO INSTEAD, I STOOD OUTSIDE MCQUEEN, AND STARED AT THE SPRING COLLECTION. IT COULD HAVE BEEN MY MOOD, BUT IT FELT SO ALIEN TO ME.
THE LINES WERE SIMPLE, THE COLORS WERE BEIGE... I DIDN'T RELATE TO THE CLOTHES LIKE I USED TO. IT WAS THE FIRST TIME HE HAD EVER LET ME DOWN.
I COULD HAVE MOPED THERE FOR HOURS, AND JUST LET MYSELF REVEL IN HOW BAD I FELT, HOW I HAD BOUGHT INTO A WORLD I DIDN'T EVEN UNDERSTAND--
BUT THERE WAS SOMEONE WATCHING OVER ME.
YOU KNOW THEY'RE CLOSED, RIGHT?
I QUIT MY JOB THIS WEEK.
I CAN'T EVEN KEEP A STUPID RETAIL JOB.
FINALLY, THE WORDS I HAD KEPT TO MYSELF BEGAN TO FORM, AND I LET THE LAWYER IN.
I CAN'T GET OVER THE THINGS I DID TO THAT GUY, AND THE TEACHER IS STILL IN MY HEAD, AND I DON'T KNOW HOW TO GET BETTER. THEY'RE EVERY-WHERE.

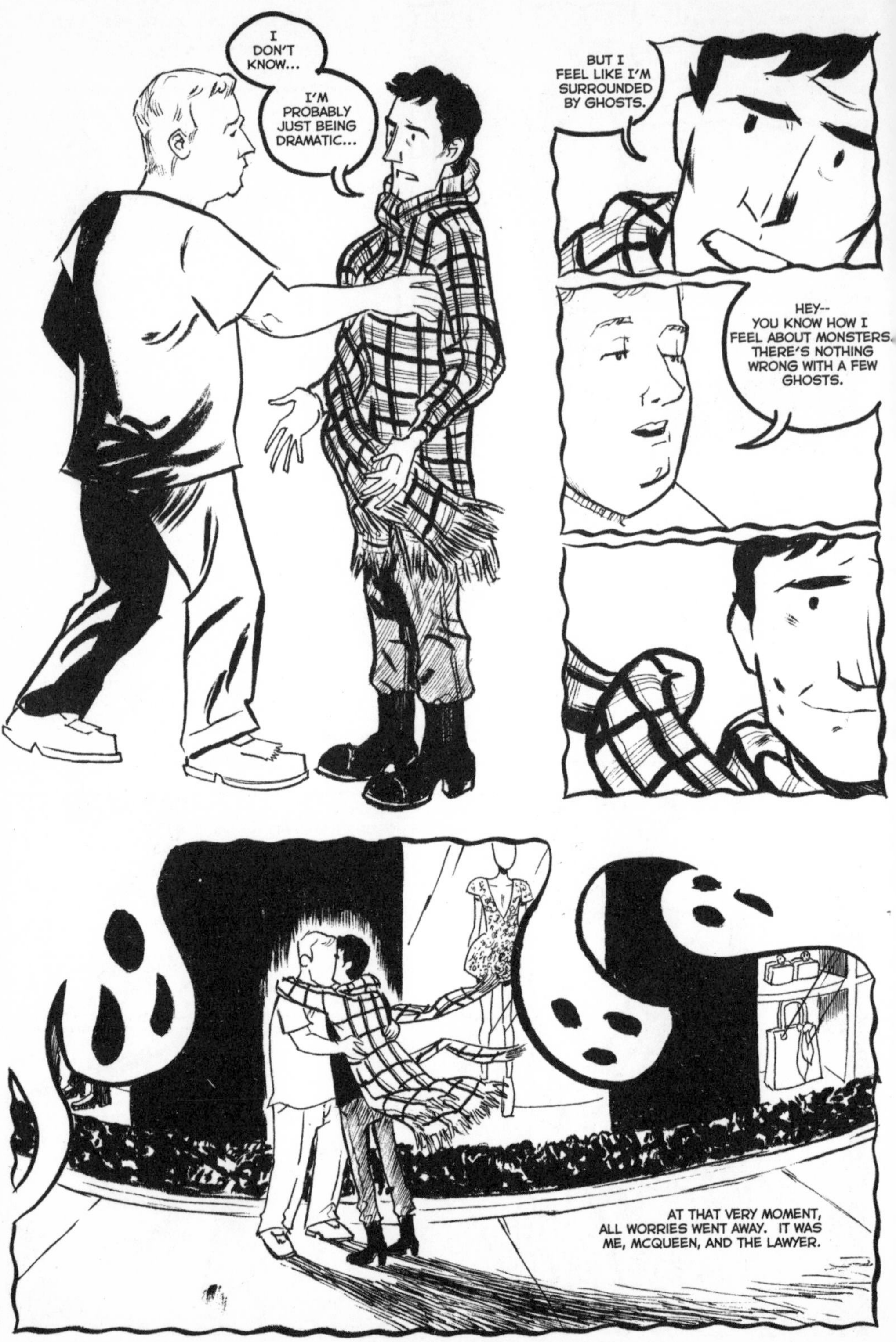
I DON'T KNOW...
I'M PROBABLY JUST BEING DRAMATIC...
BUT I FEEL LIKE I'M SURROUNDED BY GHOSTS.
HEY-- YOU KNOW HOW I FEEL ABOUT MONSTERS. THERE'S NOTHING WRONG WITH A FEW GHOSTS.
AT THAT VERY MOMENT, ALL WORRIES WENT AWAY. IT WAS ME, MCQUEEN, AND THE LAWYER.

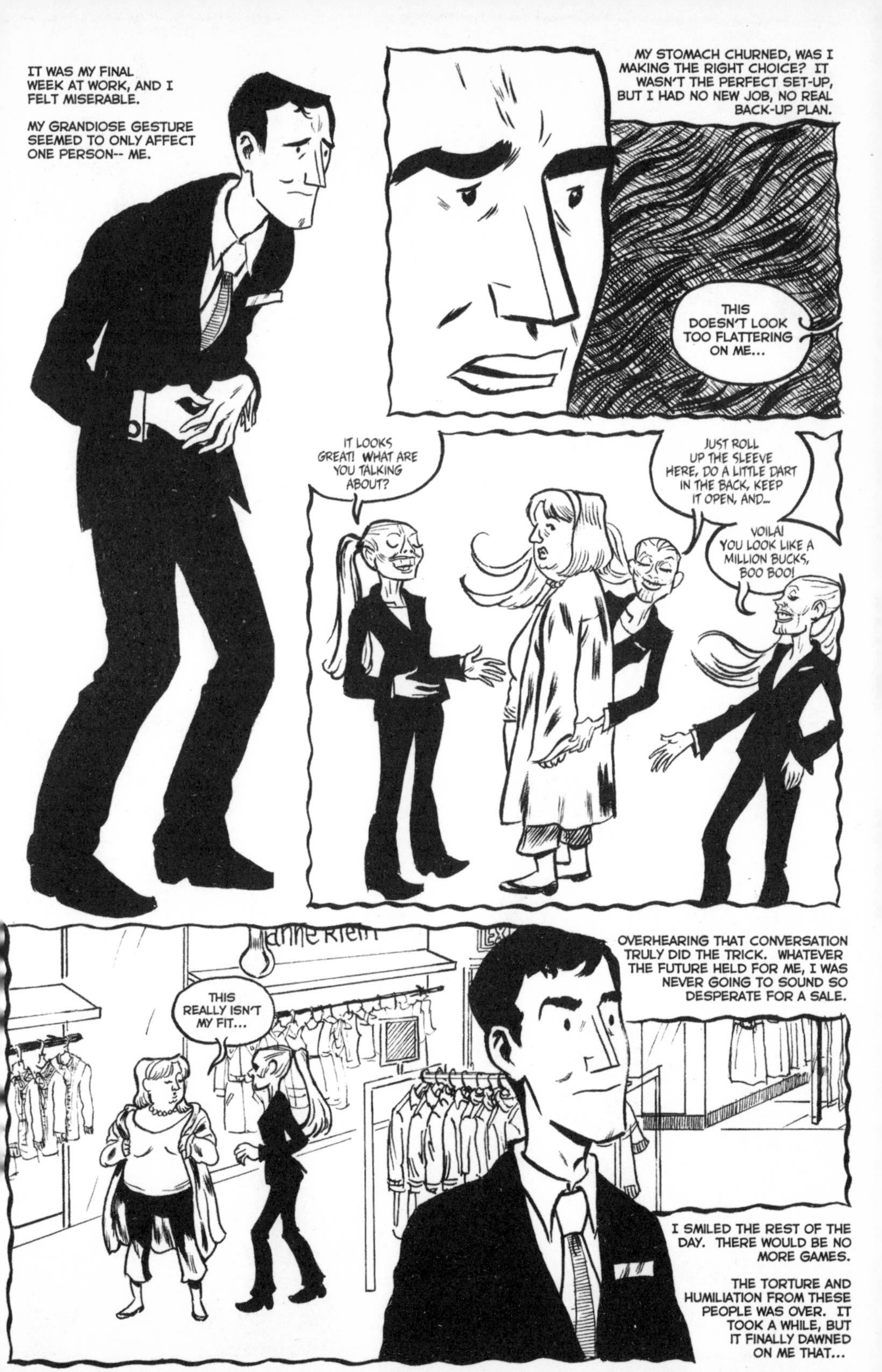
IT WAS MY FINAL WEEK AT WORK, AND I FELT MISERABLE.
MY GRANDIOSE GESTURE SEEMED TO ONLY AFFECT ONE PERSON-- ME.
MY STOMACH CHURNED, WAS I MAKING THE RIGHT CHOICE? IT WASN'T THE PERFECT SET-UP, BUT I HAD NO NEW JOB, NO REAL BACK-UP PLAN.
THIS DOESN'T LOOK TOO FLATTERING ON ME...
IT LOOKS GREAT! WHAT ARE YOU TALKING ABOUT?
JUST ROLL UP THE SLEEVE HERE, DO A LITTLE DART IN THE BACK, KEEP IT OPEN, AND...
VOILA! YOU LOOK LIKE A MILLION BUCKS, BOO BOO!
THIS REALLY ISN'T MY FIT...
OVERHEARING THAT CONVERSATION TRULY DID THE TRICK. WHATEVER THE FUTURE HELD FOR ME, I WAS NEVER GOING TO SOUND SO DESPERATE FOR A SALE.
I SMILED THE REST OF THE DAY. THERE WOULD BE NO MORE GAMES.
THE TORTURE AND HUMILIATION FROM THESE PEOPLE WAS OVER. IT TOOK A WHILE, BUT IT FINALLY DAWNED ON ME THAT...

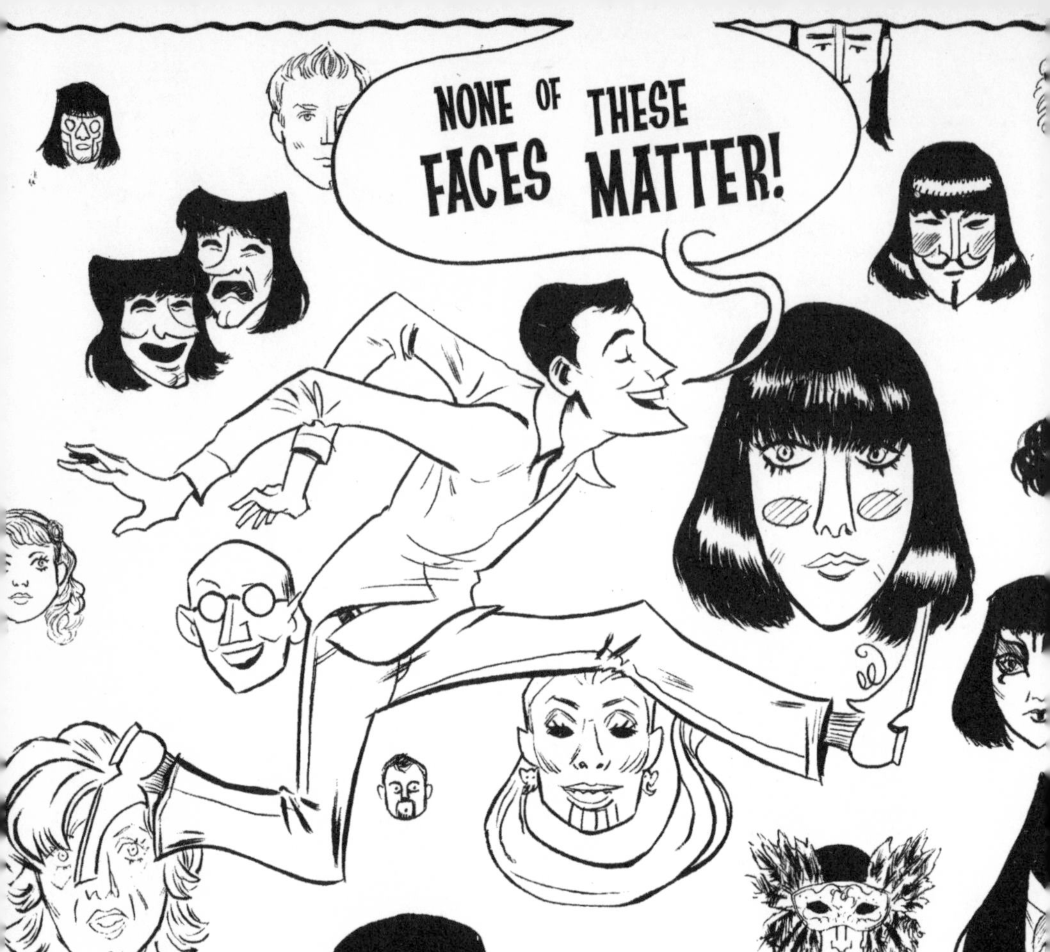
NONE OF THESE FACES MATTER!

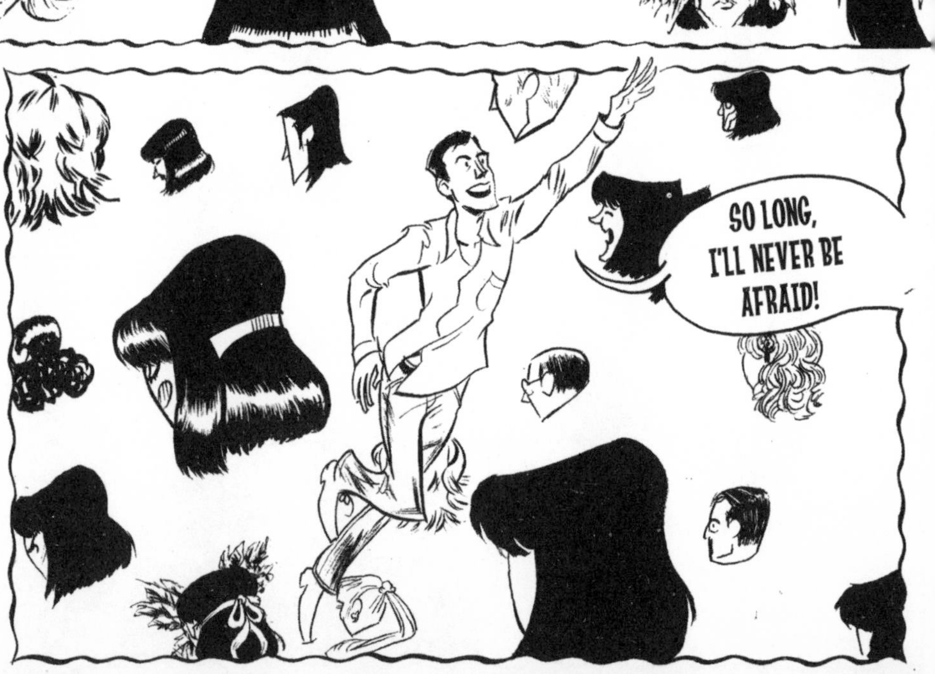
SO LONG, I'LL NEVER BE AFRAID!

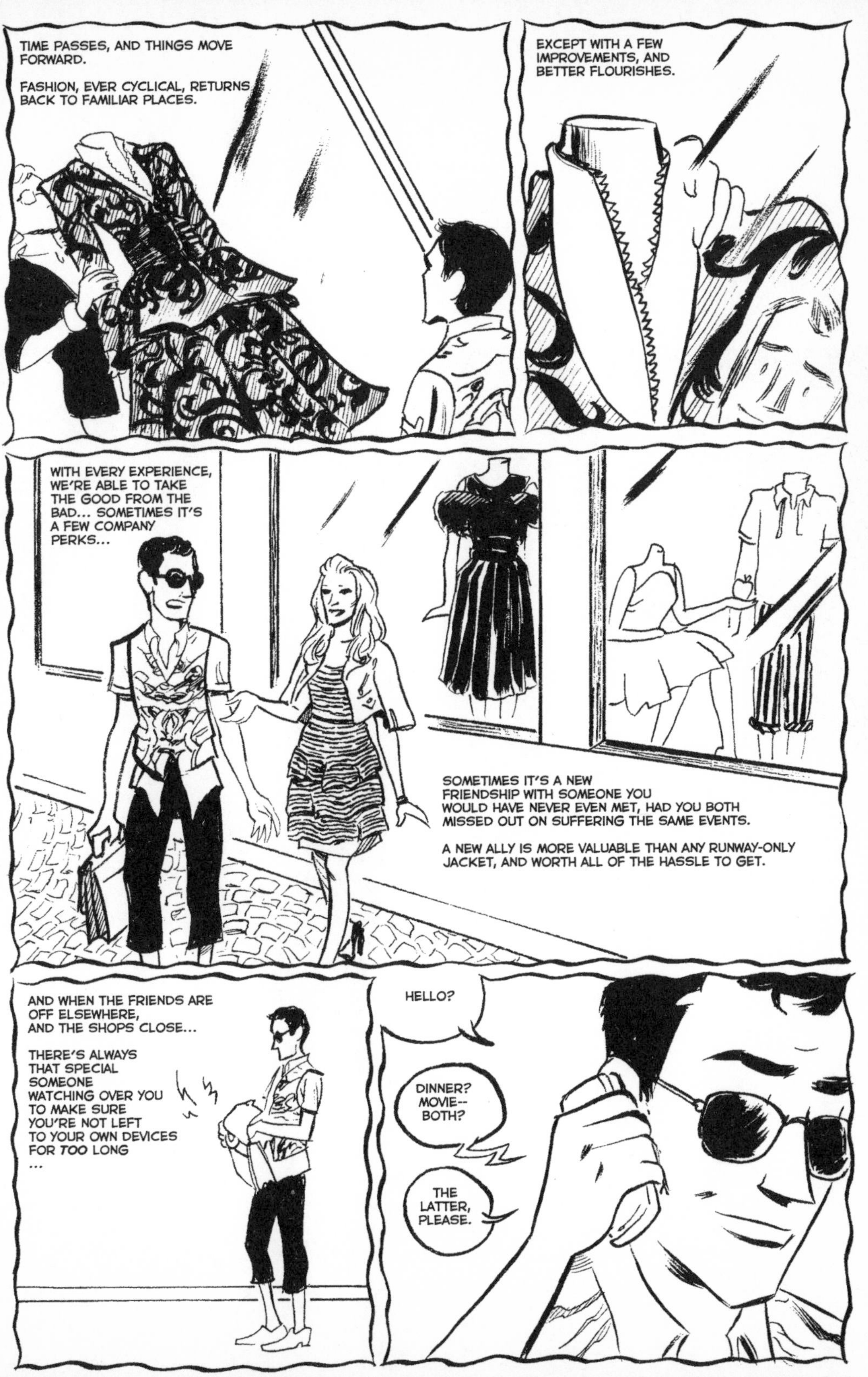
TIME PASSES, AND THINGS MOVE FORWARD.
FASHION, EVER CYCLICAL, RETURNS BACK TO FAMILIAR PLACES.
EXCEPT WITH A FEW IMPROVEMENTS, AND BETTER FLOURISHES.
WITH EVERY EXPERIENCE, WE'RE ABLE TO TAKE THE GOOD FROM THE BAD... SOMETIMES IT'S A FEW COMPANY PERKS...
SOMETIMES IT'S A NEW FRIENDSHIP WITH SOMEONE YOU WOULD HAVE NEVER EVEN MET, HAD YOU BOTH MISSED OUT ON SUFFERING THE SAME EVENTS.
A NEW ALLY IS MORE VALUABLE THAN ANY RUNWAY-ONLY JACKET, AND WORTH ALL OF THE HASSLE TO GET.
AND WHEN THE FRIENDS ARE OFF ELSEWHERE, AND THE SHOPS CLOSE...
THERE'S ALWAYS THAT SPECIAL SOMEONE WATCHING OVER YOU TO MAKE SURE YOU'RE NOT LEFT TO YOUR OWN DEVICES FOR *TOO* LONG ...
HELLO?
DINNER? MOVIE-- BOTH?
THE LATTER, PLEASE.

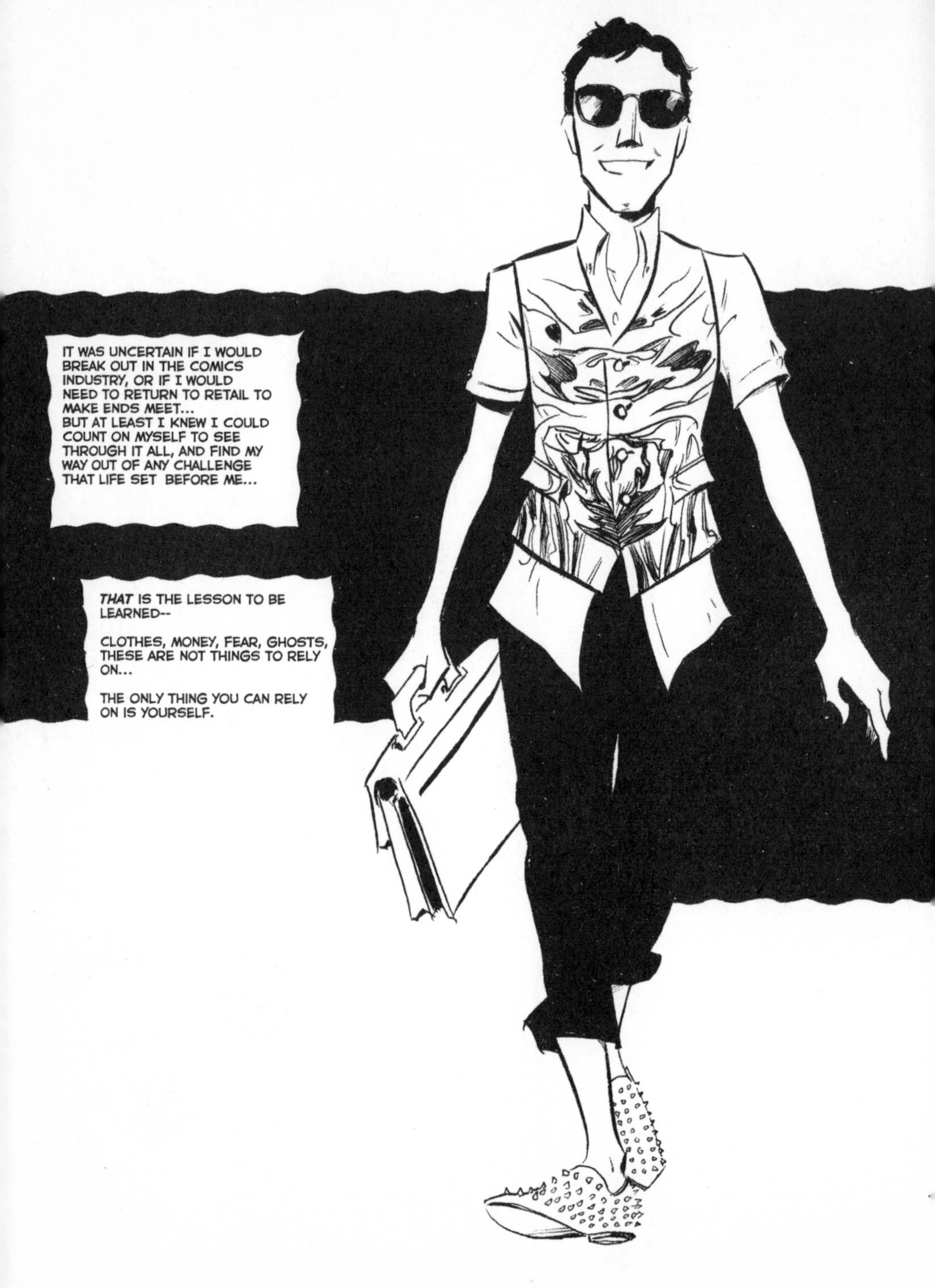
IT WAS UNCERTAIN IF I WOULD BREAK OUT IN THE COMICS INDUSTRY, OR IF I WOULD NEED TO RETURN TO RETAIL TO MAKE ENDS MEET...
BUT AT LEAST I KNEW I COULD COUNT ON MYSELF TO SEE THROUGH IT ALL, AND FIND MY WAY OUT OF ANY CHALLENGE THAT LIFE SET BEFORE ME...
THAT IS THE LESSON TO BE LEARNED--
CLOTHES, MONEY, FEAR, GHOSTS, THESE ARE NOT THINGS TO RELY ON...
THE ONLY THING YOU CAN RELY ON IS YOURSELF.

the
end

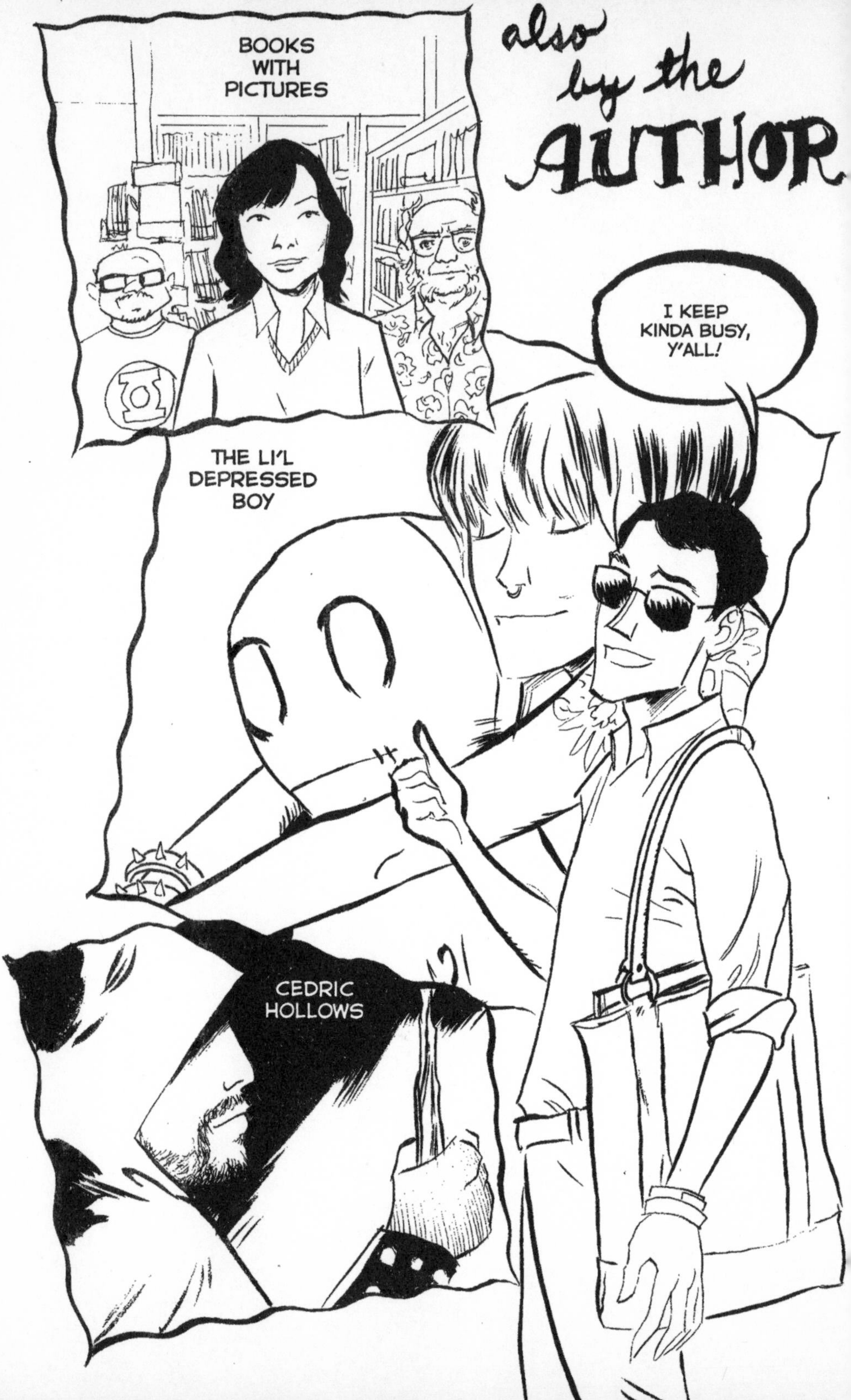
also by the AUTHOR
BOOKS WITH PICTURES
I KEEP KINDA BUSY, Y'ALL!
THE LI'L DEPRESSED BOY
CEDRIC HOLLOWS

Acknowledgements

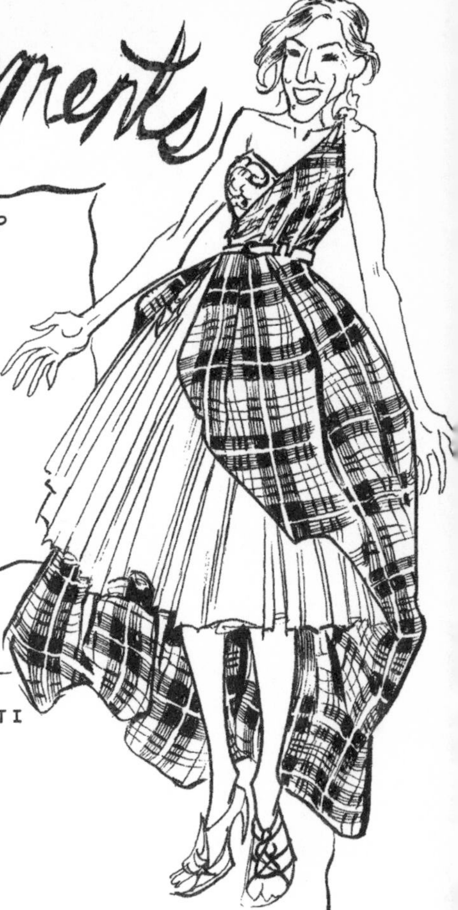

THIS BOOK WOULD NOT HAVE BEEN DONE WITHOUT THE HELP FROM THE FOLLOWING PEOPLE:

SPENCER ALCORN
HARRIS MILLER
S. STEVEN STRUBLE
AMBER BENSON
MIKAEL SEBAG
POURY GRACE
SALOMEH GRACE
DANIEL FREEDMAN
SANAZ YAMIN
SYDNEY NICHOLS
SHAWN KIRKHAM
CHRIS REGISTER
DEVIN FLANIGAN
RENAE GEERLINGS
BEN ACKER
CAMILLE CAMPBELL
MICHAEL GRACE
BRAYDEN MARC LEBLANC
JUSTIN HALL
GREG RUCKA
ROBERT KIRKMAN
BENOIT HECQUET

THEN THERE ARE THE PEOPLE WHOSE SUPPORT I CANNOT LIVE WITHOUT:

JOCELYN BROADWELL
DAVE GOLDSCHMID,
BRYAN CARPENDER
GABRIELLE ROUSSOS
ASHLEY SERRA,
CLAIRE BENNETT
NICHOLAS D. BRANDT
& ISABEL REYES

THERE ARE ALSO THE MUSES THAT KEPT ME WORKING, EVEN WHEN I WAS READY TO GIVE UP:

ALEXANDER MCQUEEN (DUH)
CRAIG THOMPSON (CAN'T YOU TELL?)
PAUL POPE
EDWARD GOREY
YVES ST. LAURENT
EMILY HAINES
SARAH JESSICA PARKER
CHANEL
BRYAN FULLER
BELL HOOKS
CORY WALKER
RYAN OTTLEY
BALENCIAGA
& ROLAND BARTHES

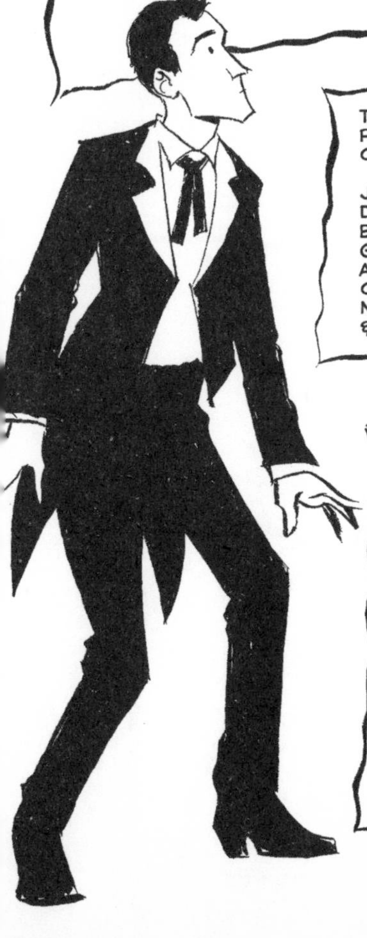

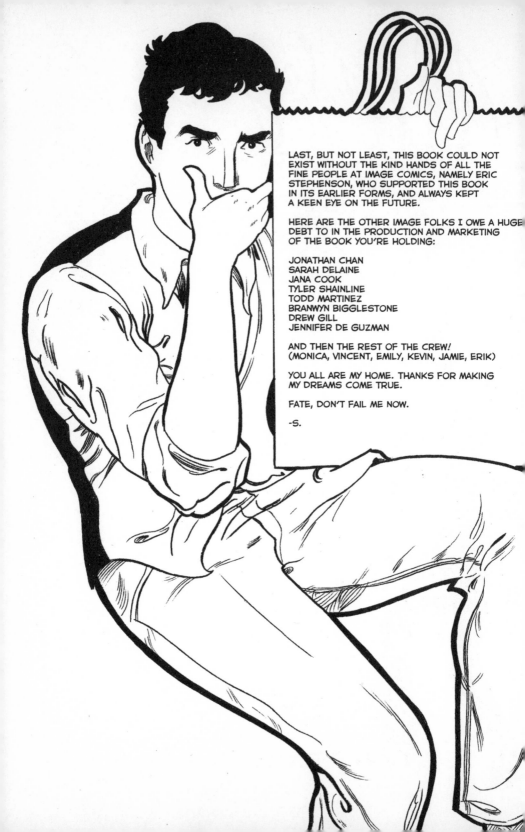

LAST, BUT NOT LEAST, THIS BOOK COULD NOT
EXIST WITHOUT THE KIND HANDS OF ALL THE
FINE PEOPLE AT IMAGE COMICS, NAMELY ERIC
STEPHENSON, WHO SUPPORTED THIS BOOK
IN ITS EARLIER FORMS, AND ALWAYS KEPT
A KEEN EYE ON THE FUTURE.

HERE ARE THE OTHER IMAGE FOLKS I OWE A HUGE
DEBT TO IN THE PRODUCTION AND MARKETING
OF THE BOOK YOU'RE HOLDING:

JONATHAN CHAN
SARAH DELAINE
JANA COOK
TYLER SHAINLINE
TODD MARTINEZ
BRANWYN BIGGLESTONE
DREW GILL
JENNIFER DE GUZMAN

AND THEN THE REST OF THE CREW!
(MONICA, VINCENT, EMILY, KEVIN, JAMIE, ERIK)

YOU ALL ARE MY HOME. THANKS FOR MAKING
MY DREAMS COME TRUE.

FATE, DON'T FAIL ME NOW.

-S.

Sina Grace is the author and illustrator
of the indie mini-series Books with Pictures,
the neo-noir Cedric Hollows in Dial M For
Magic, and the autobiographical one-shot,
Self-Obsessed.

He acts as the artist for S. Steven Struble's
cult hit, The Li'l Depressed Boy, and provided
illustrations for Amber Benson's middle grade
book, Among the Ghosts. His art has been
used by various musicians, including Rilo Kiley,
Childish Gambino, and Common Rotation.

He lives in Los Angeles, where he can be
found in coffee shops working on whatever
the next thing may be.